"Any golfer would enjoy this book, and I challenge any non-golfer to resist its wit and charm. The pleasure of reading it is almost equal to the pleasure of playing golf with Printer Bowler, perhaps not the best golfer I've ever played with, but the very best company. The book places you in a foursome, right beside him on the tee."

—*Award-winning actor* JOHN LITHGOW

"More than ever, fans and players are benefiting from insights into the essence of sports as a means to greater self-realization. *The Cosmic Laws of Golf (and everything else)* offers timeless wisdom and fascinating exercises that anyone—from duffers to pros—can use to achieve new dimensions of personal mastery through the game of golf. The focus and imagination here are similar to the Zen qualities I've been teaching in professional basketball over the past decade, and you get the feeling Printer knows what he writes. I found *The Cosmic Laws of Golf* entertaining and enlightening in ways that broadened my awareness of what's possible."

—PHIL JACKSON, *head coach of the Los Angeles Lakers*

ALSO BY PRINTER BOWLER

SPIRIT OF MONTANA

WHEATFLOWERS—RECIPES FOR LOVERS

PRINCIPLES OF NATURAL HUSBANDRY FOR DRYLAND
  GRAIN FARMING

WRITING NATURALLY

THE COSMIC
LAWS OF GOLF

(AND EVERYTHING ELSE)

PRINTFR BOWLER

 BERKLEY BOOKS, NEW YORK

B

A Berkley Book
Published by The Berkley Publishing Group
A division of Penguin Putnam Inc.
375 Hudson Street
New York, New York 10014

PRINTING HISTORY
Berkley trade paperback edition / March 2001

The Penguin Putnam Inc. World Wide Web site address is
     http://www.penguinputnam.com

Library of Congress Cataloging-in-Publication Data
Bowler, Printer.
       The cosmic laws of golf (and everything else) / Printer Bowler.—Berkley
     trade pbk. ed.
         p. cm.
       ISBN 0-425-17830-7
       1. Golf—Anecdotes. 2. Golf—Philosophy. 3. Golf—Psychological
aspects.   I. Title.
       GV967 .B68 2001
       796.352—dc21   00-049401

PRINTED IN THE UNITED STATES OF AMERICA

10 9 8 7 6 5 4 3 2 1

I DEDICATE THIS BOOK TO ONE

I KNOW AS SNOW ANGEL,

A MAGNIFICENT BEING OF LIGHT

AND A GRACIOUS LIVING

CONFIRMATION THAT LOVE IS

THE WAY TO PEACE AND HAPPINESS.

THANK YOU.

IN THE EAST, MEN ARE NOT EMBARRASSED TO SPEAK

OPENLY OF THE SELF. BUT HERE IN THE WEST,

SUCH PIETY MAKES PEOPLE UNCOMFORTABLE.

THAT IS WHERE GOLF COMES IN.

—Bagger Vance
from *The Legend of Bagger Vance* by Steven Pressfield

Contents

Preface

AS I SAT quietly one morning, in mild amazement at all the unusual but refreshing ideas filtering onto these pages, my heart had a little talk with me:

"We're writing this book for *you*. But not just you. Make it available to others who, if they wish, can take part in our experiment, our journey. It's wide open, kid, no limits but what you bring to this game. Endless opportunities for you to discover more about who you are and what works best for you. What works for you works for me, for everyone.

"That's what this is all about, finding out what you can count on in this world where, by my design, everything is evolving in continuous transformation. Bring this book into being. *Live* it. And don't take it too seriously—have some fun! Open up and stay loose, kid—this is just the beginning."

I have to mention this, so you'll understand I'm *not* posing as one who has everything figured out, here to shower you with the final scoop. Far from it. My pleasant task is to remind us (myself most of all) of a few essential verities that in our hearts we all know, but sometimes forget. Some potent new ways to make love with the auld game. Actually, they're older than the hills—they just need to be "re-discovered" and repackaged from time to time.

I'm just another fairway farmer, sharing links tales with you like golfers do everywhere while we seek and play ourselves through this enchanting game. I wish us all an enlightening, fulfilling journey as we slash though the gorse and hit all the shots on our common quest to be the best we can be.

Acknowledgments

THANK YOU...

I'M HONORED TO celebrate this fine rainbow of friends who are present here in the best of what comes through me. . . .

Grandpa Burley Bowler, a country newspaperman who instilled in me, by his kind and patient example, an enduring love for the spirit of the game and the virtues of a true gentleman. Grandma Maud who, 'til just before she moved on at eighty-six years old, walked the two miles to the Scobey golf course, pulled her cart for a brisk nine holes, then walked back home and cooked up incomparable homestyle gourmet for her boys in the print shop.

My dad, Larry, who let me play golf in between the drills and disciplines of his boot camp, and whose tremendous gift of "infinite knowledge" I'm still unwrapping. My mom, Beth Marie, who showed me, year in and year out, how love truly is the answer to every question. My awesome sons, Barley and

Liam—I want to be like these guys when I grow up!

Nathaniel Blumberg, true compadre, a living definition of grace and friendship whose grand passion and compassion for life have chipped me out of the gorse in more ways than can be measured. Thanks, Coach.

Kim, my heart embodied as a beautiful angel, flying with me headlong into the unknown, renewing our faith in life's promise and the pure joy of being home again. Sleep in a dish! *(Ich liebe dich!)*

Todd Schlapfer, extraordinary model of the finest you can be, whose healing light restores peace and joy in countless lives, especially mine. Elle and Michael, divine sweethearts, whose pure spirits help me return to what is real and shed what is not. Jerry and Beverly, who cradle this world in their arms and make you feel blessed to be alive.

Terry and Linda Bell, for so graciously helping this dream come true. Gary E. (M. le Cosmíque), what the best of America and being a real man is all about. Fellow Alien John L—master of laughter, a hole-in-one in human form, sweet and powerful as pistils in a wild rose.

Frog Miller, true amigo, for sticking with me since time began; WH Wood, for handing me a copy of *Golf in the Kingdom* back in 1975; The Criper, been there and still keeping the dream alive; Mark Ogle, "hear the words, watch the feet"; Larry Pirnie, how to grow up and still chase rainbows; Greg Raymond, my "self-esteem coordinator," for keeping me inside the white stakes; Sonny Gratzer, for his rare alchemical gift of transmuting pain into laughter; super teaching pro Johnny Yacobellis, for showing me how to relax; master teacher Scott Lefevre, making golf a better game for anyone lucky enough to find him; Het-Bob, molecular golf dude who putts with lightning bolts; Mac Schaffer, the finest worm rancher I ever met; Chris the Saint, a totally seismic experience in life as a one-liner; Larry "Sam" Schaefer, school-days golf pal, for giving me my first look at world class.

Steve Cohen, president and founder, and the hearty members of the Shivas Irons Society, where golf is played in all its transcendent possibilities.

A very special thanks to Steven Pressfield, master storyteller, soul pal, a true gentleman, for his immeasurable inspiration and generosity of spirit.

And all my blessed inner dæmons, for showing me what I've created and for hounding me to trade them all back in for love.

Introduction

For Whom the Putts Fall

WHEN I WAS thirteen years old, I spent one of my happiest summers helping Grandpa restore the abandoned nine-hole golf course near my hometown of Scobey, Montana.

He and his friends had carved it out of cow pasture during the boom years of the twenties, but it fell dormant during the Great Depression and World War II. The rolling prairie turf soon reclaimed its domain, pushing up through those roughly hewn fairways till the last man-mowed blades of grass leaned over and melted back into the earth.

Remnants of the oiled sand "greens" and tee boxes were slowly bursting apart as thistle and ragweed toiled patiently to digest them into native soil again. Here you could still sense the residual footprints of Assiniboine hunters who chased down antelope on foot not many years before this ancient sod lost its first scalp to a niblick.

We mowed and raked and dug away most of each day, buffeted by relentless winds, cheered on by meadowlarks, pestered by mosquitoes and ignored by the ubiquitous grasshoppers, challenged by scampering ground squirrels whose holes held many a golf ball and many a divot from Grandpa's mashie. In a spew of squatters' rights expletives, he'd hurl that club at them with all his might, but I never saw him actually pitch one of those little fellas up to gopher heaven.

Later each afternoon, he'd pull out the rest of his vintage goosenecked clubs and we'd "inspect the day's work." It was then he patiently taught me the rudiments of the game and I quickly fell under its spell and promise.

Today I carry to each round the memory of my golf origins born in Grandpa's reassuring presence, when the prairie breezes spun their ancient stories around my ear, when I felt the first pulse of the game calling me out to explore and unravel its mysteries.

EVEN before I shipped out to Vietnam, it occurred to me there had to be more harmless ways to get what you want. So many lives were being ruined simply because others held such gnarled visions of life's possibilities. One person looks at a pretty piece of countryside and enjoys the nice view. Another looks at it and starts scheming up a hostile takeover.

What causes one to enjoy and the other to destroy? They both come in a *Homo sapiens* package—so where are the differences located? This was one of those mysteries I felt held the secret to a lot of events happening on this planet. Even the game of golf.

By the time I came home from the war, my secure old world

of blacks and whites—deeply imprinted on my childhood psyche by countless Roy Rogers movies and Dad's Horatio Alger stories—had been churned into a mottled gray. Properly disillusioned and confused, I headed for sanctuary in the good Montana dirt. There I spent the next decade curled up in Mother Nature's bosom as she nurtured my fields of organic wheat and taught me the secrets of worms and transmutation.

But the questions wouldn't go away: What causes the fat shots, sweet shots, duckhooks, shanks, OB's, birdies and double bogeys of golf and everything else we do? Where's all this coming from and why aren't we all happy and shooting par?

I set upon my quest in earnest, gobbling up volumes on psychology, philosophy, spiritual and religious teachings. I attended lectures, workshops and private gatherings. I had nothing to say. It was a time to observe, listen.

While other people's ideas provided some helpful insights, the only teachings that felt true to me had one precept in common: Above all, know thyself. To thine own self be true. In knowing yourself, you will know all life.

That sounded right, but I wasn't exactly sure what it meant. So I set about figuring out how to "know" myself.

EVENTUALLY I found the practice of meditation proved very helpful. Being still and listening to my native voice soon gave me a sense of "knowing" that I am, like most everyone else, I suspect, a spirit being on assignment here. My job, I discerned, is to act out what I believe is true with whatever means of expression I brought with me.

My assignment also requires that I learn the laws, rules and regulations that govern life on this planet. These I've come to know as cosmic laws. They're called "cosmic" because they govern everything that exists and happens in any given cosmos ("a complete, orderly system"), such as this one in which we live.

As I began to observe life through the lens of these laws, I could see how their use or abuse determines the relationships we have with ideas, each other, and all the games we play.

The Law of Attractions, for example, states that the thoughts and feelings you hold about others *automatically compel* that same energy to affect you in a like manner. This bit of insight helps one appreciate the great wisdom of the Golden Rule—it's to benefit the *one who does* as well as the one done unto.

Outside the law, golf becomes a renegade that steals our dreams and buries them in the wilderness of anxiety. Within the law, it's a fascinating course that can lead to self-realization—as it turns us inside out, it reveals what we *really* believe about ourselves and shows us where we need to make peace in our world.

A FEW years ago, I became intrigued with the idea of how cosmic laws work within the game of golf. Being a dedicated student of both, I knew they were perfectly synchronized at some level. But how exactly? I began jotting down theories and ideas for experiments. I began meditating on how to go about this task. I started applying some of these laws to every aspect of the game I could imagine.

I soon found them to be far more than lifeless, abstract concepts. Cosmic laws are dynamic high-potency energy seeds whose job is to sprout their amazing magic through anyone willing to give them the opportunity.

As they began performing wonders right before my eyes, I'd pump my fist and hear myself gasping, "Oh my God, these things actually work!"

On these pages is a record of what I've experienced and therefore *know* to be true. Like you, I can't really verify anything simply by reading or hearing about it. They're only words and ideas until we *experience* them by acting them out. Then they become our own true knowledge, living wisdom we'll know forever.

I invite you to use what I've gathered here to demonstrate and confirm these laws for yourself. Some may take a lifetime to fully appreciate and apply, while others yield their gifts more readily. All are tremendous opportunities to revolutionize your golf game and the rest of your life, as you wish.

THIS is my humble offering to golfers everywhere as we, kindred seekers all, continue to court the mystery and harvest the simplicity of golf. At our sides are my old friends, the meadowlarks and prairie winds, who keep coming by to remind us: It all comes down to enjoying this divinely inspired game and the fine people we play it with.

I hope your stroll through the fairways of this book brings you many pars and much satisfaction. Have a fine round.

You're Very Likely to Enjoy This Book If . . .

. . . YOUR INTEREST IN the game isn't limited to scores, handicaps, stroke-saving gimmicks, golf carts and an obsession with swing mechanics. You know, like: one-piece takeaway, left or right arm straight, turn shoulders but keep head still, supinate hands as weight shifts to outer side, set club parallel at the top, then turn hips and start down smoothly on the inside while shifting weight back to the other side, keeping eyeball glued to golf ball, pronating hands as you clear hips through impact—all this while you're trying so hard to relax you feel a severe sphincter seizure knotting up because there are so many things to remember that your jammed-up brain desperately explodes into a confusing array of paralyzing contradictory signals through your rapidly contorting body, which, by now, is slashing at the ball and gasping in frustration at the aerodynamic anomaly that probably just occurred. Whew!

As billions of synapses collapse into the groan heard round the golf course, you tell the cart girl to make that a triple with a twist of lime. Better anesthetize those anxieties to prepare for the continuing mind-blown-into-matter experience of the next shot.

Not that those aren't perfectly valid approaches to playing golf. After all, we need some harmless ways to express our deep angst at popping into a world where our own masochistic tendencies keep hacking apart our fledgling visions of greatness. It's the confounding paradoxical human condition for which sport, golf in this case, mirrors us so well.

We're not here to talk swing theory or techniques, equipment, or course management—all of which are very important and are best discussed with your teaching pro. I'm assuming you already know or are taking qualified instruction on how to make a good swing through the ball, how to chip and putt, etc. Proper training in the fundamentals of golf is helpful, but not essential, to take advantage of the information in this book.

Our concern is about *consciousness management* and a higher dimension of tremendous potential you can unleash into your present game. We have some fascinating tools here that can make each journey from tee to cup a much more creative, illuminating experience.

So if the endless rounds of quick fixes and frustration are wearing you to a frazzle, and what oughta be is usually better than what is . . . then it might be time to inject some new life into the old dog and lift off in a new direction. To where?

To the discovery, for the serious student, of an immense source of power and perfection that has been waiting only for your call to come forward. (The only prerequisite for having these powers is that you were born.) To the re-awakening of your native ability to manifest anything you can imagine for yourself and your golf game. To assuming your rightful mastery over the dimpled white sphere of every experience in this fascinating, bewildering game called *being alive*.

It's high time to replace the fear of change with a renewed sense of adventure and anticipation. Let's try something new and see what happens!

This invitation is in perfect accord with our job assignment to this planet, which is to realize our finest visions and share them with the rest of the world. While the job description is simple, carrying it out is, like golf, a lifelong test of our determination to get our minds and bodies to cooperate with our dreams.

It's a daily challenge that often makes me wonder if I've learned anything at all. Want to give the gods a good laugh? Just think you know something. So let 'em laugh—I'm a fool for golf and happy to prove it anytime.

Yet I find comfort in knowing that while our human condition is always changing, cosmic laws are always the same—so at least there's *something* we can count on.

We can also count on this simple truth: Our own highest visions are self-propelled divine energy beings, waiting for our permission to come in and play their miracles through us. They'll do all the "work" if we let them—the harder we "try," the more we jam up their path to our success.

Real success is natural, effortless—energetic and dynamic, yes, but without the fatigue of stress and struggle. *It's supposed to happen all the time.*

One of our biggest challenges is to stop grinding, leave our busy brains in the parking lot, and simply *allow* our ideals to work out through us, as they are intended to do.

If you think such things are possible or impossible for you, then you're in perfect condition to swing on through these pages. Please join me as we take the auld game out on the cosmic links and see what she can do.

Inside the Kingdom

TO BE SURPRISED,

TO WONDER,

IS TO BEGIN TO UNDERSTAND.

—José Ortega y Gasset

Mystical Questions, Magical Answers

HOW DO YOU hole a feathery in the dark of night, the way Shivas Irons did in *Golf in the Kingdom*? How did the legendary Bagger Vance stop the cosmic clock and make three quick holes-in-one from more than two hundred yards out, with a one iron no less? (You don't think those stories are fiction, do you?)*

*The two greatest books on golf ever written, I humbly submit, are *Golf in the Kingdom* by Michael Murphy and *The Legend of Bagger Vance* by Steven Pressfield. These intriguing tales of miraculous experiences re-awaken the wonder at life's limitless possibilities and the joy of renewing our own quest for what is real and enduring. The book you are reading now contains the seeds of *how* such magic can happen for anyone. You can argue with them or laugh at them. Or plant them and watch in amazement as ancient mysteries reveal themselves right where you're standing.

Or, of perhaps more immediate interest, how can we regular folks break out of our limitations and get some miracles into our own games?

Everybody's got some answers. As you can see—in the burgeoning supply of golf books, magazines, videos, websites, schools, instructors, and free advice from playing pals—the tips and "secrets" are changing all the time. Some brilliant new insight may suddenly revolutionize your game . . . until things start falling apart a few days or rounds later.

But all that can change if you're breathing and willing. In this kingdom, physical dexterity is second to innocence of heart and expansiveness of mind.

We're dealing here with what always works and never changes. Now

> The key is not to look anywhere for yourself, but to find yourself everywhere you look.

that's a presumptuous statement to be sure, but true nevertheless because it's based on cosmic laws that were, are, and forever will be. They govern all life—our every thought, feeling, word and deed—even golf. If you believe that is possible, you might ask: What are these laws and how do they work? How do we use these seemingly abstract concepts to create a happy golf game?

My mission is to propose, for your consideration, some proven and useful answers to these questions. Better yet, may you discover many of your own answers as we amble through this short course on how to apply the fruits of Self-discovery to the playing fields of golf. Our first assignment is: Prepare to take full command of the universe within. And, in doing so, become the master of all.

As we begin our journey into the realms of self-mastery, let's briefly peek into some kindred kingdoms where mysteries are unveiled and success is natural.

With cosmic law, what's true for one is true for all.

THE EYE OF THE FISH

A FEW THOUSAND years ago in ancient India, a man's stature often was measured by his accomplishments in the sports of the day, much as it is even now. Chief among these was the bow and arrow, one of history's longest-running instruments of human self-projection, not to mention self-destruction.

Perhaps the most famous archer up to Robin Hood's time was a princely fellow, a paragon of old Indian culture named Arjuna. A man of renowned physical dexterity and spiritual attainment, Arjuna was the chief disciple of Krishna, who is to the Hindu faith approximately what Christ is to Christianity. A classic account of the landmark conversation between Krishna and Arjuna is recorded in the Hindu sacred book, *The Bhagavad Gita.**

Each year India's finest archers would gather from all over for a national contest to determine the greatest marksman in the land. Immense prestige and honor went to the winner,

---

*From the substance of Hindu legends, I've created the following contemporary version of one of Arjuna's many extraordinary feats.

whose fame and glory would compare today with earning the coveted green Master's jacket, throwing in the U.S. and British Opens for good measure.

Hundreds of warriors would fire their arrows over the first few days, and as the contest wore on all but a handful were eliminated. As time drew near for the sudden death playoffs, waves of anticipation swept through the thousands of excited fans packed around the shooting field.

The finalists would face a much more difficult target, now being strapped to the top of a sixteen-foot-high pole about an eight iron away. The milling crowd watched in silence as a man shimmied up the pole and secured to its peak a small wooden fish about eighteen inches long. The fish was painted metallic gold and outlined in a half-inch cobalt blue stripe, with a bloodred eye about the size of a quarter.

That eye was the target, a doorway to the hall of legends to be opened only with the arrow that could pierce it.

As each finalist approached for his turn to shoot, a contest judge would sweep his arm from horizon to horizon and ask the contestant: "What do you see?" A variety of answers came forth: Some archers noted the throngs watching, others saw the pole, the fish, the sky, the sun, the green hills on the horizon, virtually everything visible to the human eye. After describing their view to the judges, they were allowed to step up and fire one arrow at the target.

Arjuna, the reigning champion, had the honor of last to shoot. By the time he took his position, none thus far had hit the fish's little red eye. The fish had lost a few scales, but its unscathed eye still stared back at the crowds with an other-worldly, almost defiant gaze.

A soft breeze wafted through the mass of excited onlookers, who at this point were still as stone. You'd have thought that Nicklaus was surveying the putt he needed to win his seventh Masters.

The judge then turned to Arjuna and asked: "What do you see?"

Without hesitation, Arjuna replied: "I see the eye of the fish." He then turned to face the target and slowly drew back his arrow.

His face was calm yet shimmering with intense concentration. His mind was like a flat, glassy pool of still water, empty of all thought. Only his simple intention to merge with the target occupied his consciousness.

Arjuna's eyes now bore like a laser beam instantly locking in to the tiny red dot in the distance. For a moment he stood motionless. Then suddenly his arrow was streaking along that beam until it drove deep into the eye of the fish. . . .

How was Arjuna able to strike the fish's tiny eye with such unerring assurance? What special skills did he have that the others apparently didn't have? From a distance his feat appears almost miraculous. But from inside his being, the view was very simple and uncomplicated.

Beneath the magical sheen of his accomplishment, he was simply demonstrating many of the cosmic laws we'll review in this book.

WHAT IS ZEN AND WHO IS PYTHAGORAS?

SOME OLD ZEN masters are quite the jokers. They'll tell their aspiring students things like "the definition of Zen is that it is beyond definition, and even that is questionable." Which helps one understand why Buddhist monks traditionally shave their heads—they'd be tearing their hair out if they had any.

For those of us who'd like to keep what hair we have, perhaps we at least can agree on some understanding of this "indefinable" yet fertile spiritual practice. Simply put, Zen is a process of evolving our attention out of the human mind's mechanical, conditioned, reactive state into the soul's intuitive, freewheeling, natural way of life. It's a destination and the journey itself that leads one into the infinite free energy world where anything is possible and dreams come true instantaneously.

This is more than possible—actually, it's everyone's destiny.

To use the puny human mind to try to comprehend why we're here and how we can get some real satisfaction is like trying to dig a gold mine with a golf tee. It's like looking to a child's fun-with-numbers book in hopes of understanding zero gravity and the Theory of Relativity. Our brain tool is utterly insufficient and way out of its class for tasks like that. To depend totally on the human mind is to be locked in a small closet, unaware of the rest of our universe.

Thus, the Zen goal of "mindlessness" would have us open our eyes to a much

When I'm hungry, I eat.

When I'm tired, I rest.

This is wisdom.

—ZEN MASTER TO ONE WHO ASKED THE MEANING OF ENLIGHTENMENT

grander vision of who we are and what we're doing here. One of the Zen teacher's first tasks is to show you how futile it is to use an inadequate tool (your mind/brain computer) to do an almost impossible job (understand your life).

A common teaching method is to give the student a *koan*, a spiritual riddle that can be solved only in the heart consciousness. You may be familiar with some of these classic koans: *Who are you before your parents were born? Where is your mind not? What can be known only by not knowing it?* These don't make much sense, of course, but they're not supposed to.

Only the sense-less heart, free of the mind's dead-end logic, can reach into the spiritual plane and decipher the wisdom hidden in these riddles.

But it's not about the riddles. It's about coming home to your heart.

PYTHAGORAS,* the Greek master who ran an esoteric mystery school in Croton, Italy, around 500 B.C., had some interesting ways to measure how well his students were attaining the goal of "mindlessness." One way was to give them three problems that could only be solved intuitively, not by mental logic. When his students could "solve" these problems, Pythagoras knew they had reached a dimension of consciousness where only those solutions are possible.

For the curious among you, here are Pythagoras's three problems. A few years ago I worked out the first one, but to this

---

*Many are familiar with the Pythagorean theorem that the square of the hypotenuse of a right triangle equals the sum of the squares of its two other sides. He offered many other profound gifts to our planetary storehouse of spiritual yet very practical treasures.

day I'm not sure how I did it. Anyway, when you get rained out, give these a shot.

With only a compass (the kind that draws circles) and an unmarked straight-edge ruler:

1) *Trisect an angle:* Divide any angle into three equal angles.
2) *Square a circle:* Draw a circle, then make a square the same area as the circle.
3) *Double a cube:* Create a cube, then make another cube twice the volume of the first.

Talk about hair-pullers! Note: I'll ship a dozen of your favorite golf balls to the first one who sends me a clear solution to any of those three problems.

AT some point, as one turns more to the heart's intuition and less to the limiting human mental world, a state of enlightenment or cosmic consciousness is reached.

Enlightenment simply means a true understanding that you are God, and so is everything else.

This is the goal of Zen and all true spiritual teachings of the world.

It doesn't necessarily mean that the nature of this world changes. As Pulitzer prize–winning poet Gary Snyder said: "Before enlightenment, chop wood and carry water. After enlightenment, chop wood and carry water."

It means we see other beings as part of ourselves, through eyes that include rather than exclude. We understand our purpose

The human mind is like a computer, filled only with the programs and data we've put into it. Its ultimate message is: "Don't ask me for understanding. All I can tell you is what you've already told me."

here is to serve the greater good of all, not just our little body-identities. We lose interest in creating impressions, and enjoy the freedom of being a self-sufficient nobody who can be anybody or anything it wants to be.

The good news is that these various degrees of enlightenment can happen anywhere, anytime. You don't have to go to some esoteric mystery school (other than this one called Planet Earth), or live in a monastery, or sit in a dark cave with a serene grin on your face. Attaining a manner of enlightenment can happen anywhere you are, no matter what you're doing.

By the time you play your way through this course, you'll have some timeless shots in your bag to help you become as "enlightened" as you like.

RETURN TO THE KINGDOM WITHIN

ONE OF OUR most Zen-like, cosmic golfers is the young Severiano Ballesteros. We could pick from dozens of players who've inspired us with their gifts and amazing feats, but the young Seve perhaps best represents the magic of innocence and imagination that many of us spend our lives seeking to recapture.

We've heard the stories of how Seve learned the game, beating an old five iron around the sandy outskirts of Pedrena, Spain, learning to create whatever shots he needed with the limited equipment available to him.

He was young and, like most of us in our youth, hadn't yet learned to make excuses for missing a shot (bad lie, distracting noise, too windy, back hurts, not enough appearance money, etc.). A missed shot was a teacher, pointing out a new opportunity to learn. None of the conditioned self-destruct programs had taken root in his curious, open mind.

His only interest was: How can I pull this off? And he was the living answer, perfectly wrapping his imagination around every situation that arose. He was caught up in the exciting world of possibilities—he could do anything he wanted. Why not?

You are what you believe you are.

—SEVE BALLESTEROS

During those early years, starting with his first British Open victory, he *could* do almost anything he wanted. Like an excited child, his heart was pumping with the thrill of adventure and discovery—not the nagging doubts that later would plague and hinder him.

Where did these doubts come from? How did they take root and siphon off the joy and excitement he once exuded?

We are either creating new dæmons or reacting to old ones, depending on where we invest our attention.

Creating keeps us from reacting because it's impossible to do both at the same time.

How could he rid himself of these dæmons* and return to the innocence and curiosity that make golf an exhilarating experiment, rather than a painful trek through the netherlands of despair?

Someday, somehow I know Seve will return all his dæmons to the heart-fire whence they came and reign as champion of himself once again. As we're all destined to do.

But for his unusual talent and savvy with the game, Seve's story is our story. We all share the same challenges, agonies and ecstasies we express through our golf games and other activities of slightly lesser importance (home, family, business).

How can we re-discover the magic of a youthful, innocent heart?

Some turn to religion, others to fortune-tellers, some attend self-help seminars, many opt for mail-order gadgets that promise less strokes and more sanity . . . and a few decide to re-create their world with a new team of friendlier, more helpful dæmons.

---

*Dæmons are entities (thought forms) we *create*, individually or together, by nurturing a thought or idea until it seems to take on a life of its own. They become part of our beings and influence the way we think, see and act. Dæmons need our attention, our vital force, to survive—withdraw it and they dissolve into free energy again. Good or bad, they show us the great power we have in our use of an ancient law: As you think, so you are.

GO FOR DAYLIGHT!

JUST TAKE YOUR best shot and go for wherever you see daylight, whatever truly works and gives you more than fleeting satisfaction.

This particular go-for-daylight course was specially designed by our expert team of merciful Fairway Angels. The "mercy" part derives from a deeply compassionate attitude they've acquired after noting the high degree of misery and frustration emanating from golf courses around the world.

Our Fairway Angels mapped out the "Rub o' the Green" and "Cosmic Golf Training Exercises" to show serious students a way out of the gorse into lush emerald fairways of excellence and real satisfaction.

By "serious student" we mean: Do you *really* want to be a more successful golfer, or are you secretly content in just fussing over the flaws and foibles of your game?

> Educating the mind without educating the heart is no education at all.
>
> —ARISTOTLE

This is not a path for those who seek comfort and security, but for hearty souls willing to cast off into the unknown in search of the ultimate prize.

The journey to self-mastery is mysterious, rampant with the hazards and bunkers of our own dæmons—a thrilling challenge to the sincere seeker, a confounding maze of obstacles and torment for the idly curious.

Our quest is about returning to the innocence of childhood, letting go of the bogey attitude in our brains, and being willing to experiment with some new (actually ancient) visions of who we are and what we can be. It's about leaving behind forever the wearisome hypnotic spell of self-defeat and delusions of impotence.

The kingdom truly is within, and that's right where we're headed. Because that's where the real work gets done, where the birdie eggs are laid before they hatch into birdies on the golf course.

This how-to manual is a course map for what could be one of the most mind-boggling golf excursions of all time, an odyssey of re-creation from which you might never return.

Got your gear ready? Let's drop by the Cosmos Country Club and check out the local rules. . . .

Rub o' the Green

THE SOUL PURPOSE OF THE UNIVERSE IS TO SEE THAT,

SOONER OR LATER, WE EXPERIENCE OUR EVERY DREAM

COMING TRUE — EVERY THOUGHT, FEELING,

AND BELIEF WE HOLD AS OUR OWN.

IT DOESN'T CARE WHAT WE DREAM.

ITS JOB IS TO LET US SEE AND FEEL THE WORLD

WE'VE CREATED WITH OUR CHOICES — AND THEREBY

SHOW US THE WAY TO FREEDOM.

Cosmic Laws of Golf

THE GODS PROVIDE. WE DECIDE.

THE COSMIC LAWS of Golf are universal and apply to every activity: golf, work, thinking, talking, mowing the lawn, making art, making love, making money, hauling the garbage, whatever you think, say and do.

I present them as background information to use with the training exercises and, subsequently, on the golf course. At first glance, some may not appear to relate immediately to golf because their domain includes all that is. But I assure you, as a friend once reminded me, that "all wisdom is in the heart o' the game and may be used there most fruitfully."

The one principle from which these and all other laws arise is the Law of Love. As I use it here, Love is a name for the foundation substance of the universe, the infinite presence of pure energy from which all life is created, sustained, and transformed.

The seven cosmic laws we're about to review are facets of the Law of Love, like rays emanating from the sun. They describe the way things work in this world. Like gravity, they're in effect twenty-four hours a day, like it or not. We can ignore or fight them, which most people do most of the time. Or we can work with them, which some people do some of the time—and enjoy golf as an exciting exercise in self-discovery rather than a frustrating foray into self-defeat.

Take the Law of Polarity (cause and effect), for instance. It's generally agreed that swinging mostly with the arms over and down across the ball usually causes a slice or a pull, depending on how your clubface arrives at impact.

You can ignore this and keep slicing/pulling the ball, groaning every time. You can fight it by trying to steer the club into alignment and getting a stunted but occasionally straighter bunt somewhere out there closer to the hole.

Or, instead of trying to patch up the effects of a bad swing, you can find what *causes* you to come "over the top." Change the cause and the effect *automatically* changes.

Like scientists who use laws of physics to create impressive things like computers and spaceships, you can use the laws of metaphysics* to create a golf game equally as amazing and functional.

These laws and exercises won't fit in your quick-fix gimmicks bag. They aren't feel-good pills for instant relief, but

---

*Metaphysics—the physics of energy outside the range of human sensory perception.

What does your forever look
like?

proven, verifiable tools
that provide expansive
new options for your pre-
sent and future game. To
get them working, all
they require is a bit of
your attention and willingness to let them play through you.

As the training exercises reveal, it's all about using our native
powers to create *an illuminating new dimension of our old game*. Every
moment is an opportunity to imagine and act out a fresh version of what we want to be now.

Cosmic law offers essential instruction in the art of consciously re-discovering, re-creating, re-defining ourselves—'til
our highest ideals and current realities are indistinguishable.

This is the work of the ages. And it's going to take forever—
because that's how long we'll be around in one form of energy
or another.

What does your forever look like? What occupies the space
between the ideal and the reality of your game? What must
change *so your ideal can become your reality?*

Let's get to it and find some *real* answers to those questions.

If this sounds too metaphysical and unlikely to be realized in
your life, you may enjoy taking a quick peek at these Cosmic
Laws of Golf and the training exercises that follow. Just for the
fun of it.

NOTE OF CAUTION: Once you review these laws and
work through the exercises, the way you see golf may be
changed forever.

Cosmic Laws of Golf

(and everything else)

Law of Polarity
cause and effect

Law of Attractions
thoughts are magnets

Law of Perceptions
as you wish, so you see

Law of Intentions
place your order

Law of Commitment
cement the back door shut

Law of Spontaneity
instantly act on your voice

Law of Acceptance
eliminate self-defeat

You must swing smoothly to play golf well.

And you must be relaxed to swing smoothly.

—Bobby Jones

Law of Polarity

EVERYTHING HAPPENS BECAUSE SOMETHING CAUSES IT TO HAPPEN.

EFFECT IS A CHILD OF CAUSE, AND WE'RE THE PROUD PARENTS.

THE LAW OF POLARITY* describes how the world as we know it began and continues to be. It's about cause and effect, the reason things happen the way they do. Most importantly, this law determines why our golf ball goes where it goes. Get a grip on this and the rip will follow.

*Note: Our brief review of Cosmic Laws begins with this most essential one. It's pregnant with helpful insights for the sincere, persevering student of the game. Mega-tons have been written around this subject, probably because it's the key to everything that ever happened (including golf) since time began. For some, it may seem like playing a 7413-yard TPC course from the tips. No worries! Just bring your own game and the shots will come. Right now I'm talking to you from somewhere out on the sixth fairway during a very humbling yet exhilarating workout.

To assume the correct grip, we need to loosen our white-knuckled clenching of the club, resume normal breathing, and start at the beginning. I mean, the *very beginning*. . . .

Before the universe was split into pairs, there was no beginning or end, day or night, woman or man, right or wrong, plus or minus, high or low, yes or no, good or bad, fast or slow, big or small, black or white, within or without, past or future, pain or pleasure, balls or cups, hooks or slices.

Legend is that The Primal One (God, if you like) grew lonely because, while it was everywhere, it was all by itself. It was aware of itself only as being no*thing*. No thing but pure undefined energy existed throughout its entire being.

To appreciate Primal's predicament, go outside to high ground on a clear day, lie flat on your back and gaze up into the sky. It doesn't take more than a few moments of staring into that infinite blue beyond to start feeling very spacious. In some cases, an unnerving disorientation can occur when you have nothing to see but nothingness.

Try this and you may get a small sense of how Primal was feeling—like a little kid standing in the middle of the Sahara Desert and lamenting, "Hey, there's nobody here to play with!" Nothing but one infinite field of static, but very conscious and self-aware, energy—in a manner of speaking, this was God's condition before we started showing up on the first tee.

As an experimental cure for this absolute aloneness (all-oneness), Primal One created two fundamental ways of being: the masculine and feminine. The result is what some people call "The Big Bang Theory."

These primary energy prototypes also are known as

Alpha and Omega, yang and yin, positive and negative—polar opposites that, when joined in balance, *create a miniature of the Primal One.*

To ride herd on this new idea, Primal created the Law of Polarity, which gives these masculine and feminine energies a powerful, built-in urge to join and become whole again. Each is designed to attract and merge with its compatible mate. This law is the basis of sexual attraction, but it isn't limited to males and females. It's Primal's universal force of *re-union* built into every kind of being and energy field from quarks to quasars.

Primal designed these opposite but complementary energies so they could combine, grow, disintegrate and re-form into numberless combinations ranging from simple subatomic particles to complex things like DNA molecules, human organs, girls, boys, relationships, starships and galaxies.

The need for individual beings and things to combine with their "other half" is one of the most irresistible and compelling forces in the universe. The golf ball (masculine) and the cup (feminine) are no exception.

The masculine and feminine polarities also are key players in what we call "cause and effect"—how a change in one polarity causes changes in the other. Primal asked Sir Isaac Newton to record this idea in his Laws of Motion: every action causes an *equal* and opposite reaction. For example, when you finally keep your head still (cause), do you get a truer putt (effect)? Of course you do.

Like lovers, the plus-minus poles on a car battery, the two sides of a coin—one can't exist without the other. And when one polarity mate changes, it *must* affect the other. This law applies equally to things, ideas, people, attitudes, golf swings . . . everything.

This thumbnail sketch of "How Life as We Know It Began and May Forever Be," can help us understand the truly pressing matters, like: What causes my golf ball to land out there in a pile of horse apples next to the pink-ribboned stakes?

Let's get to the golf of the matter here.

Bobby Jones, the Pure One, gives us a perfect insight into how the Law of Polarity decides why our golf ball goes where it goes.

Because it's their nature, the masculine initiates, the feminine completes. Masculine is the cause, feminine is the effect. When out of balance, the masculine drive to overpower creates the effects of wars, poverty, slices and shanks. Where it's in balance, peace and many pars are found.

Bobby said: "The impulse to steer, born of anxiety (cause), is accountable for almost every really bad shot (effect)."

To "steer" the club is to micromanage the swing by consciously trying to guide the clubhead into a square position at impact, rather than trusting a smooth swing through the ball. Steering is a fine example of how frustrating and tiring it is to try to change an effect without first changing its cause.

Until we truly resolve the *root cause* of anxiety—regardless of how much mental patching and swing tinkering we do—it will fling its chaos into every shot we take.

You can try curing anxiety with sedatives, analysts, psychics, pep talks from friends and other sources of free advice, and swing doctors. They may offer temporary relief, but no reliable solutions to that deep gut-churn that keeps sending frantic panic signals through your nerve endings down the shaft into your quivering clubhead.

Those interim remedies never have worked and they never will because they deal only with effects, not the fundamental cause of anxiety, which is *fear*. . . .

Fear of changes, fear of not being enough, fear of failing, of succeeding, of not being loved, of being meaningless, of looking weak and stupid, of being outside the circle of cool people, of losing what you have, of losing control, of not getting what you want—and greatest of all, the fear of Self-discovery.

Like all thoughts and feelings that come through us, fear and its offspring—anxiety, panic, aggression—move our bodies and clubheads to perfectly express their nature.

But fear not! The cure is always here. It is *trust*.

Trust in what?

Trust in your own validity and purpose here, the truth that you (and all of us) are created as a unique and essential ingredient in the whole recipe of Primal's plan.

Trust that *you* are creating your experiences—as a way your soul has chosen to teach you about your choices and beliefs.

Trust that Primal's plan is for your peace and happiness, not your pain.

Trust that everything that's rightfully yours is here or on its way to you now . . . no need to push, shove, or force anything, including golf shots.

Trust that you can improve your golf and everything else by revitalizing your beliefs and self-images (causes), rather than trying to "steer" how they *must naturally express themselves* (effects), just as a mirror must reflect precisely the image that informs it.

The nut of it is: Trust that if you let go of worrying and pushing, what naturally will occur is the pure expression of your Primal self—the perfect native you that is free to come out and play after all the old fear garbage gets hauled out of the way.

Primal, our real self, doesn't want us to hook or slice, shank or hit it fat.

> The profound wisdom and power behind these three magic words—Let It Go—have cured more illnesses, restored more relationships, and inspired more birdies than all other means and methods on this planet.

The fear/anxiety filters we've created and allowed to act in our systems are causing those problems.

Let them go by understanding that those old filters are only role options *you've chosen* to play: victim, aggressor, loser, hero, duffer, martyr, powerless pawn, power dude or whatever. No matter who else does what, each of us is personally responsible for accepting the beliefs—our current set of self-image filters—that drive and shape our lives. (See *Law of Attractions, Law of Perceptions.*)

And we can rewrite our personal movie script, escape from our filter-cage, and cast ourselves as any character we want, anytime we want.

How do we "let go" and do an effective rewrite? I've found it takes four important steps:

- First, clearly identify the conditions (effects) you no longer want in your life. Identify their causes, the fears and anxieties that create those conditions. Ask yourself what they are, and listen closely.
- Be *willing* to set yourself free. This can be tricky because sometimes, when it gets right down to it, you may find you prefer the misery of the known to the mystery of the unknown.
- Imagine the ideal you (no worries, making birdies, enjoying yourself?). The easiest way to give up something old is to start something new. Do you believe this "new you" is possible? If so, continue to next point.
- Accept and commit to your new vision and *start acting like it's true.* See it no longer as something you want to be, but as something you *now are.* When you truly believe, the power of your commitment will manage the operational details in all kinds of synchronistic and magical ways. (See *Law of Commitment.*)

If you aren't getting the results you expect, take a gut-check to see if you truly want it because: *You always get what you accept and believe you are.* Wishful mind chatter is no match for the mighty power of our true beliefs. And understanding the difference is what this track is all about!

When we finally decide to disengage from fearful old self-limitations, the world soon starts reflecting our new way of being.

Now your golf teacher will have a much easier time getting through to you. You'll assimilate instruction much more quickly and thoroughly. Your handicap may start falling. You'll run out of excuses because they'll be so obviously irrelevant.

Every condition is present in our lives because our soul is *using* it to teach us about our choices. Whether it's about slicing, caving in under pressure, bad relationships, anything . . . first ask: "What am I using this for?" A response always comes, often immediately. If we accept our answers, the condition is then free to evolve and resolve naturally.

The swing slows down, white knuckles take on their natural color again, the gut stops churning.

We can finally relax, as Bobby Jones suggests, and swing smoothly.

HERE'S one way I used the Law of Polarity to resolve, as Bobby observed, "the impulse to steer, born of anxiety."

A few years ago I'd managed to squeeze into a nine handicap, but my game had gone bad to the point I was getting exhausted from fretting and trying to fix things too much. One day when some friends and I went to play a course in Montana's Flathead Valley, I resolved to give up fighting and trying so hard.

Just before we started, I had a little conversation with myself:

"To hell with worrying—it's too much work and too boring. I'm going to relax, just play some golf. It doesn't matter if I screw up. My goal is fun and peace of mind, not numbers on a card. I'll do my best, give up the rest, and let the score be whatever it is."

I guess I really was ready to "give it all up" because I immediately felt more at ease than I had in weeks. I then birdied the first hole, and the next, and ended up with a 2-under 70—the first time in my life I'd broken par for eighteen holes.

Finally preferring to trust my intention and allow it to play through me (cause)—rather than caving in to panic and anxiety—set the tone for the round and yielded a career best for me (effect).

Once I took the priority off needing to score, I scored well. Once I was willing to let my fun-and-peace goal run free to happen on its own—rather than hounding myself with worry—it *did* happen. The numbers were coincidental, a sweet by-product.

Of course, we don't get a career round every day, but laying down all the worries dramatically increases the odds of surpassing our par potential and enjoying some peace of mind.

It doesn't take long to prefer self-trust in letting go over the self-torture of fear and worry. Do it and you'll probably get hooked.

HERE are a few more practical and down-to-earth ways to use the Law of Polarity:

Consider seeing yourself as an adventurer, an explorer, an innocent child brimming with curiosity to discover new possibilities of what can be. Keep *seeing yourself becoming and acting out* what you want to be. These new images become new causes that will begin manifesting satisfying new effects, naturally and effortlessly.

Consider dropping any remaining pretenses of being sophisticated, all-knowing, better or worse than anyone else. Be just who you are at the moment, and stop dragging around all those cardboard cutouts of your imaginary pseudo-selves. Go where

Ye see, the basis for a change in the way a person plays the game must be laid in his entire life.

—SHIVAS IRONS IN *GOLF IN THE KINGDOM*

nobody but you can go—and don't spend more than a nanosecond being concerned with what anybody else thinks about your behavior. That is, act like you're free—because you truly are free of everything but yourself.

Those are huge steps to a relaxed, smooth golf swing.

You'll find out how much more intriguing and capable you've become now that you're more interested in who *you are*, and less concerned with who you aren't.

MOST of this business can and should occur before you even get to the golf course. So by the time you're lacing up your spikes and hauling out the bag, you'll have the anxiety part of the equation near zero balance.

Among its many gifts, the Law of Polarity offers golfers two clear choices:

- *Cause*: Anxiety
  Effect: Nerve-shearing meat-grinder frustration golf

or

- *Cause*: Trust (in letting our old dæmons go, which gives our highest intentions the freedom to come out and play)
  Effect: Our *authentic* game with no fear and anxiety

The Training Exercises (especially *Being Still* and *Who's Calling Your Shots?*) reveal ways to use the Law of Polarity to remove the root causes of bad golf shots—and let your native plan emerge, the perfect game your soul created long, long ago.

THOUGHTS ARE THE TOOLS PRIMAL USES TO CONSTRUCT

EVERY LAST DETAIL OF THE UNIVERSE,

FROM THE GRANDEST GALAXIES

TO THE WAVE PARTICLES OF THE SUBATOMIC WORLD.

AS MINI-PRIMALS, OUR THOUGHTS AND BELIEFS DETERMINE

THE SHAPE AND QUALITY OF EVERYTHING FROM OUR

OCCUPATIONS AND RELATIONSHIPS

TO THE NUMBERS ON OUR SCORECARDS.

Law of Attractions

THE MATERIAL WORLD IS A MATHEMATICALLY PRECISE REFLECTION OF OUR INNER
THOUGHT WORLD AND BELIEF SYSTEM. WE CREATE AND RE-CREATE OURSELVES BY
THE BELIEFS WE CHOOSE TO HOLD AND NURTURE.

THE LAW OF Attractions is the twin sister of the Law of
Polarity. It governs our physical, mental, emotional and spiritual worlds. This law is precise and without exceptions.

Ours is a world of magnetic fields constantly attracting their
likenesses to themselves. Thoughts literally are magnets.
Intensity of feeling and conviction behind the thought determines the *power* of the magnet.

Laws of physics and metaphysics require that the thoughts
we hold (cause) *must* attract their likeness (effect) into our
worlds, each according to the power we give them.

Our thoughts create exact mirrors of themselves that appear to be "out there" looking back at us—through people, things, conditions. A slice or duckhook (effect) appears out there as *an exact reflection* of our desire to overpower and force the ball (cause).

When the desire to overpower is replaced with a more relaxed and trusting attitude, likewise that will produce a golf shot in its image.

Our beliefs (our most powerful thoughts) determine how we experience everything that happens in our world. And, among our beliefs, *the strongest ones win every time*. What we hold to be really true in our heart and gut naturally dominates all other lesser thoughts and weaker convictions—no matter how much we try to "talk" ourselves into anything else.

For instance, if you're nerve wracked about a crucial shot you're about to make, but hold a stronger belief that you can pull it off, you'll pull it off. If you don't believe, you won't.

The Law of Attractions also reminds us that we can give thoughts immense power. Accepting any negative idea with even a second or two of attention lets it sweep in and swell the ranks of our existing anxieties. There, teamed up with its old pals, it can really make fools of us.

Some of you may relate to this familiar tale of woe:

I was very nervous because one of my favorite golf guys, Gary McCord, was in our group of scramble teams playing a late-afternoon derby one fine day at Eagle Bend GC near Big Fork, Montana. I was feeling big pressure to not blow it for my team, trying way too hard to play at least decent in front of all these good players. I saw another guy, suffering from the same sphincter convulsions as I, miss a ten-*inch* putt to eliminate his team.

So it's my turn to drive on a long par three, wheat field on the right. Sweating with worry I pull out my three iron and say to myself, "For God's sake, don't hit this sucker OB!"

Even before I said it, I'd let the thought sneak in where it quickly grew fat on my basic fears until, by the time I hit the shot, it unerringly accomplished its mission—my ball was sailing over the fence posts into the yawning sod.

My teammates were staring at me with sickly, forced smiles, telling me it was okay, quietly thinking what a disgusting loser I was. The Law of Attractions got me good that time!

Talking to your fears—saying "don't" or "do"—only feeds and roots them deeper in your mind. My OB fear was my strongest belief at the time and it had no choice but to play itself out into my physical world.

Thoughts are tricky little diggers and we have to control them with constant vigilance . . . or they'll have their wild and wiggy way with us, as you can see by observing the state of human affairs on this planet.

Another facet of this law came to me from an old farmer— actually a wise spiritual master dressed in a seedy old straw hat and bib overalls—who once told me: "Don't be too concerned about answers, my boy. You can have all of them you want.

"You're living in a world full of answers to questions asked long ago and being asked right now."

Then he leaned forward and in a hushed voice said, "It's the question that's the key, young man. You must learn what questions to ask, because you'll *always* get an answer—whether you like it or not, whether you choose to see it or not."

This conversation brought about my first awareness of the Law of Attractions and I was doing a lot of head-scratching at the time. The implications of what he said next are still ringing through my head:

"The question—that is, every thought, feeling, and conviction you're holding—magnetizes its polar opposite, the answer, to come forth out of omnipresent energy. This occurs by much the same process as our schoolroom magnet gathers the iron filings about it in precise and orderly fashion.

To find out what you really believe, look at your world.

What we each see and feel is what we are convinced is true for us. By the Law of Attractions, our own self-image (cause) is creating our present golf game and the rest of our life (effects).

"Here the magnet is the 'question' and the filings form the 'answer.' *The magnet is the cause and the filings are the effect, so to speak.* The question actually creates its own answer, much as the magnet creates the field that holds the iron filings in place. You see what I mean?

"You and your thought world are also a magnet, ever-changing yet constantly creating your life in the likeness of your thoughts. You are the continuous question (cause) and your world is the continuously unfolding answer (effect). It's simply impossible for it to be otherwise."

I stumbled out of that conversation with a freshly scoured brainpan and that queasy feeling of knowing the inevitable could no longer be avoided, that is:

I am responsible for everything that happens in my life. I am free to choose what I think and believe. My inner beliefs and attitudes determine how I experience my outer world of people, places and par possibilities.

Like planning a garden, we always have a choice between consciously selecting what seeds we plant or letting the "whatever weeds" take over and sprout their unsightly confusion all over our landscapes.

Our heart/mind garden, where we create our lives and our golf games, is exactly the same.

We're usually choosing between two main options:

- We consciously and carefully plant, nurture and harvest our own thoughts and visions, or
- We unconsciously allow the random thoughts and belief seeds of the mass mind to enter our systems and "grow" themselves through our lives.

  We either sing our own song, or some other force uses us to play its tune.

The Law of Attractions is at work night and day, answering our questions, educating us on our choices, revealing—through the world within and around us—what we really believe.

As you believe, so you are.

The training exercises (especially *Being Still, Who's Calling Your Shots?, Believe and It's Yours*) offer excellent methods by which to consciously use the Law of Attractions to get rid of the "weeds" and bring forth the true golf game that's been waiting in our wings since time began.

Mental jabber and wishful thinking are wisps of grass scattered by the powerful wind of our deep beliefs.

THE REAL VOYAGE OF DISCOVERY

CONSISTS NOT IN SEEKING NEW LANDSCAPES,

BUT IN HAVING NEW EYES.

—Marcel Proust

WE MAY NOT BE ABLE TO CHANGE THE WORLD,

BUT WE CAN CHANGE HOW WE SEE IT.

IRONICALLY, THAT DOES CHANGE OUR WORLD.

Law of Perceptions

A GOLF COURSE IS A PLAYING FIELD FOR GOLFERS, A GALAXY OF UNIVERSES FOR A MICROBE, A FEEDING GROUND AND OUTHOUSE FOR BIRDS . . . A THIN LAYER OF GRASS AND STICKS UNDER WHICH THE ENTIRE PLANET IS BREATHING.

WHAT'S THE DIFFERENCE between perception (how we see) and reality? For working purposes, let's say reality is everything we believe exists forever—like God, the Primal One, universal energy, taxes. . . .

On the other hand, perception is a limited, unique and constantly changing *point* of view that shows us only fragments of reality. Perception is the mental porthole through which we see only a small patch of the ocean.

Our perceptions edit, color and shape things to our fancy *to show us what we want to see at any particular moment.*

Among the numberless examples of how perception differs from reality is the old journalism school "objectivity test" many professors give their students. You're sitting in class and suddenly the door flies open and some strange character barges into the room, runs about babbling sensible and incoherent phrases, then runs back out the door. Everyone is left gasping and wondering what just happened.

With a smug "gotcha" look on his face, the professor now asks the class to write a news account of what just took place.

All agreed that someone ran into the room, but after that you get as many varied stories as there are students in the class. Yet so many journalists lose sight of this fundamental lesson when they go off to work in the news media. They keep telling us what "is" when they're really giving us their limited, partially informed and often highly prejudiced *point* of view.

We are billions of related but diverse individuals, each seeing our point of view through a totally unique viewing glass. We are fragments seeing fragments mixing it up with other fragments in a seemingly endless contest to see whose point of view can prevail.

The pickpocket looks at the saint and sees only pockets.

—Ram Dass

The Law of Perceptions reveals that there are two kinds of people in this world:

Those who understand that our normal perceptions provide a very limited view of reality, and those who think theirs covers all possiblities and is therefore the only valid point of view.

And . . . those who know that how we see anything *is always a choice*, and those who think they have no choice and what they see is all there is.

A fascinating use for this law is to practice new ways of seeing that yield more satisfaction than the old ways. We are always free to decide how we look at anything. The great truth here is that *how we see something determines what it is for us.*

Depending on how we choose to look at it, a golf course— or anywhere, any activity—can appear as an exciting challenge to test our character and skills, or as a gauntlet to be run through to the sanctuary of the 19th hole. A place to find out more about how creative and resourceful we can be, or an exasperating hacking tour through the murky regions of our self-defeat mechanisms.

How we see our game, our round, our next shot, the fairness or outrage of it all is governed by our *true preferences*, the filters through which we see ourselves and everything else.

True preferences are the ones rooted deep in our subconscious, that fertile garden where every thought, belief and self-image we're born with or have accepted, often unknowingly, keeps flowering into our world.

A simple way to see what your true preferences are is to stop and look at what is happening to you: how you play golf, your personal and business relationships, your convictions and belief systems, your view of the world, what you have and don't have.

All are determined simply by what we deep down *believe is true.* And what we believe is determined by what we've accepted and agreed to from a vast array of options. Somewhere along the line *we chose* what we now believe. Nothing can be in our lives unless, on some conscious or subconscious level, we ask for and allow it. That would be against the Law of Polarity, and nobody breaks that one!

An earthworm perceives digging through the dirt all day as a much more pleasant experience than going fishing.

The universe is designed to help us experience our preferences—so we can see what works for us, and what doesn't.

Prefer to find the value, the instruction in whatever we're facing and it will show itself. Prefer to see oneself as a victim and the universe obediently will present all kinds of evidence to support that point of view.

Thus, the essence of this law is: As you wish, so you see.

OUR golf game does us the great favor of revealing our true, but often hidden, preferences through our feelings, golf shots and scorecards. Don't let this scare you! Better to use this information to identify and let go of those old agreements and preferences that don't work for you anymore.

Then you can replace them with updated versions of who you want to be and how you want to play golf now.

The training exercises *Believe and It's Yours* and *Who's Calling Your Shots?* offer some highly effective methods to use this law to perceive a whole new field of possibilities for your golf game and all the other games you play.

INTENTION IS A BLUEPRINT, A "JOB ORDER"

WE TURN IN TO THE UNIVERSAL ENERGY POOL.

THE POOL RESPONDS IN EXACT PROPORTION TO

THE CONVICTION AND SINCERITY OF THE INTENTION.

THAT'S ITS JOB—AND IT DOES IT PERFECTLY.

EACH ORDER RETURNS WITH A NOTE THAT SAYS:

"HERE'S WHAT YOU SAID YOU WANTED."

Law of Intentions

THE ROAD TO HELL IS PAVED WITH GOOD INTENTIONS. SO IS
THE ROAD TO HEAVEN. TELLING THE TWO APART IS THE RUB.

A GOOD FRIEND once told me a simple, powerful way to get what I want. She called it "Placing Your Order" and it can yield amazing results on the golf course and everywhere else. Here's the idea:

Each morning, after doing what you do to wake up and cogitate, sit quietly a few minutes and do the best you can to clear your head. Now focus on your heart center and imagine a golden white ball of sun blazing away right here. Hold this a few seconds, with the understanding that this ball of sun represents your individualized Primal spirit that gives you life and consciousness.

Then say to your sun: "Here's the kind of day I intend to have. . . ." Now go ahead and "place your order" just like you would in a restaurant. On this particular menu is whatever you can imagine you want in your life. Choose what you think is nutritious, but don't stuff yourself. Remember, you can do this every day so leave a few items for tomorrow's feast.

Now that you've ordered your daily bread from the universal kitchen, the Law of Attractions will start bringing you everything—as conditions, things, people, inspirations—to fill your order.

Sometimes you become aware of this happening, sometimes it's not so apparent. Sometimes you may not understand all the implications of what you ordered up until you get it. But please know this law is working around the clock.

Important note: Don't make requirements about how your order should be filled—big mistake! Plant it as a seed in the universal energy soil, wrap it in lots of faith, and let 'er fly. Don't follow it around, worrying and trying to micromanage it. That's a sure way to stop it in its tracks. Let it be free to go blossom on its own.

Your results may not appear to come and bop you on the head, but often you'll notice new things starting to happen, some as if by "coincidence." You may notice your golf ball, even when it's slightly mis-hit, finding the target for no "reason" at all.

A few important considerations when placing your order:

1) Truly believe that you deserve and are ready to accept your order. You won't get it if you don't. (See *Law of Acceptance*.)

2) Be very specific—and think through the implications of what you want. Because sooner or later, unless you change your order, you'll get it. How your order gets filled often involves your participation—*so be ready to do your part* as ideas and opportunities show up. Order up a new Ferrari and the universal support staff will get started on it right away. But it may require you to work eighty hours a week and give up your golf game for a few years. Or it may not. Get the idea? Just be willing to participate.

3) Ordering up blessings for the good of all, rather than just for one's body-self, seems to stimulate a much stronger response from the universe's infinite storehouse. That's probably because the fundamental nature of life is to expand and share, not to contract and hoard.

4) Asking for finer qualities—like love, happiness, forgiveness, breaking 80 or par, rather than for more things and gadgets in your life—also seems to bring quicker results. If you want them, the gadgets will come, but see point 2) above.

5) Orders are always filled with the extra gift of enlightening us on where our values are. Like the guy who fervently placed his order every day simply for a beautiful woman to be his companion and lover. Soon she arrived, but he hadn't counted on her being a transvestite who insisted her two psychotic brothers move in with her, too. Nothing wrong with any of those folks—they just aren't who he thought he had invited.

You have to be very careful of what and how you order, be specific and thorough—and think through all the implications you can. Whatever you don't specify in your order, random thought energies of the mass mind will fill in the gaps with God knows what.

WHEN we use the Law of Intentions on the golf course, we can place our order at the beginning of the round, for each situation and for each shot.

Ask and you *will* receive a response that perfectly reflects the sincerity, conviction, and consciousness of your request.

Placing your order takes as much or less time and is immensely more effective than the normal approach to most golf shots: "Well, let's see what happens here. If I . . . blah blah blah." *Before* you set up on the ball:

- Firmly declare your precise intention to yourself.
- *Believe you deserve to have it come true.*
- Picture it clearly. Do this thoroughly but quickly—no need to make a big ceremony of it.
- Now let everything evaporate from your mind.

Set up, relax, focus on the target, and swing away.

Have some fun watching yourself master this simple yet profoundly effective way to release new precision into your golf game. You'll enjoy feeling your native power re-enter your consciousness and come alive in your hands.

The training exercise *Believe and It's Yours* offers some specific keys and methods to create intentions for success—and enjoy your *inherent right* to realize your every heart's desire.

THE MOMENT ONE DEFINITELY COMMITS ONESELF,

THEN PROVIDENCE MOVES, TOO.

A SYSTEM OF EVENTS ISSUES FROM THE DECISION,

RAISING IN ONE'S FAVOUR ALL MANNER OF UNFORESEEN

INCIDENTS, MEETINGS, AND MATERIAL ASSISTANCE

WHICH NO MAN COULD HAVE DREAMED

WOULD HAVE COME HIS WAY.

WHATEVER YOU CAN DO OR DREAM YOU CAN,

BEGIN IT. BOLDNESS HAS GENIUS, POWER, AND MAGIC IN IT.

—Johann Wolfgang von Goethe

THE CHOICE HAS BEEN MADE, NO ESCAPE EXITS, NO WAY

BUT STRAIGHT AHEAD—

AND ABSOLUTELY NO OTHER OPTION

BUT TO GO THERE NOW.

Law of Commitment

•TRYING• IS AN ATTITUDE OPTION THAT SAYS YOUR TIME FOR SUCCESS IS NOT NOW,

BUT IN THE FUTURE, OR MAYBE NEVER.

WE USUALLY HEAR the word commitment used in love relationships. A classic play on this theme I now quote from Christopher Buckley's hilarious "The Counter-Rules" (*New Yorker* magazine):

"When the conversation turns to 'commitment,' tell her you once witnessed an Amazonian ritual in which a shaman sewed a man's and woman's tongues together with crocodile gut. Remark, 'Now, *that's* commitment.' She'll probably change the subject."

When we talk about commitment, the conversation must include an understanding of the single-minded passion and dedication required to truly commit to something—whether a goal, a person, an idea, a job, a tournament, a golf shot. Total commitment absolutely affirms that the goal unquestionably will be achieved—and you're totally dedicated to sticking with it until it does. Anything less . . . forget it.

> The results we achieve are in exact proportion to the intensity and dedication of our commitments.

The young Buddhist acolyte was badgering his teacher again as they strolled by the river, wanting to know how and when he could become "enlightened." Finally the teacher grabbed the boy by the sleeve, pulled him into the river, plunged his head under water and held him there. As the oxygen in the boy's lungs was absorbed and carbon dioxide began bubbling into its place, he began thrashing and clawing to free himself. Still the teacher held his head under . . . until the first hint that he was about to start breathing water.

The teacher then pulled him up out of the water and let him gasp and sputter a moment. Then he said, "When you want to find God as desperately and single-mindedly as you wanted just one more breath of air, you will very soon discover this enlightenment you seek."

Commitment is an all-or-nothing deal and it absolutely rules out any possibility of failure. This is rare because, while we daydream about wanting endless things, the ideas often don't go anywhere because we don't lock them in with unshakable determination and perseverance.

Precise science governs this law, which works perfectly with the Law of Attractions. A firm, irrevocable decision establishes a powerful magnetic field that locks into place the exact quality and determination of your commitment. This magnet *literally* begins attracting all the people, circumstances, ideas, things and wherewithal to realize the goal you've cemented into place.

This same process is at work when you totally commit to a round or a golf shot.

Please understand, energy simply *has no choice* but to perfectly mirror the qualities of our magnetic field—our thoughts, feelings, ideas, beliefs, judgments, fears, loves . . . and commitments.

In most of us, our energy qualities are always changing as we entertain new thoughts and feelings, take in new information. Thus the outer world, our mirror, appears to change as it reflects our new ways of seeing.

Now take note! The unique quality of a *commitment* is that you have declared that this particular part of your magnetic field *will not change*. It will remain constant no matter what else happens because . . . you are committed. Any part of us that remains constant gathers an immense amount of energy around it—much greater than passing thoughts that flit through and gather no photons.

A fixed commitment is like a radio crystal that receives a constant inflow of energy only on its frequency. It continues gathering a powerful accumulation around the image of your commitment. (This is how, like Primal, we are constantly using free energy to create things in the image of our firmly held thoughts.)

For example, look at the difference between a casual acquaintance and a strong love commitment with a partner. How much greater fulfillment and intensity do you and your loved one bring into each

Commitment is a way to enjoy freedom from choice.

other's life? Why? For many reasons, of course, but primary among them is the force field of your commitment. The magnetic attraction of your desire and dedication continuously creates and sustains what you're really committed to. Lose that commitment and things start dissipating quickly.

Translate this law into your golf game by totally committing to your overall goals and training plan. Commit to the game you want, to each round, each shot you make. You're not out here to "see what happens." (Well, if you are, you'll surely see what the chaotic parade of random thoughts brings you on the golf course—we all know that one!)

Commitments work only when we are willing to do whatever it takes to fulfill them. And when we absolutely refuse to allow any doubts a voice in the matter. Want a ten or five or zero handicap? Make the commitment, get the right attitude, plan and allot the time to create it. *Believe* it will happen. Then act it out.

This is not a wistful mind game. It's absolute dedication of energy to realize a specific goal. Dedicate the energy, get the goal.

With true commitment, you can minimize chance and invest precise, specific goals—and specific results—into every phase of your game.

Many of the training exercises (especially *Believe and It's Yours,
The Magic Triangle, The Target Is Locked*) offer some superior, timeless, results-oriented techniques that will help you show yourself the miracles and pleasures of real commitment.

OUR BODY'S PRIMARY IMPULSE IS TO BREATHE.

WE NEVER QUESTION OR ARGUE THIS—

IT IS SO FUNDAMENTAL AND ORGANIC,

SO ESSENTIALLY NECESSARY.

OUR HEART'S PRIMARY IMPULSE

IS TO GIVE US EXACTLY WHAT WE NEED

EACH MOMENT TO ACT OUT

OUR NATIVE PERFECTION—

BUT OH, THE INTERNAL DEBATE

THAT NATTERS ON ABOUT IT

NIGHT AND DAY!

Law of Spontaneity

MEDICAL RESEARCH SHOWS THAT AS THE HEART CENTER OF THE HUMAN EMBRYO
EXPANDS, IT FORMS THE HEAD CAVITY AND CREATES A SMALL NODE THAT
BECOMES ITS BRAIN. EVERYTHING BEGINS AND ENDS IN THE HEART.

STRANGE AS IT may seem, language is a fascinating phenomenon that can lead to many birdies and occasional lunch money. My lifetime of language studies (I'm a totally unabashed wordnut) reveals several key insights that can be of significant value on and off the links.

The fundamental question of "Where does language come from?" is enough to make most people head for the bar or excuse themselves to the restroom and never come back. But wait! Understanding the source of our language can reveal where our golf shots come from—and help get the shots we want rather than those we don't want. Worth a look?

As you'll see in the exercise *Who's Calling Your Shots?*, our minds are filled with voices coming into our awareness from a variety of sources. Many of these voices—from the planetary thought-junk humankind is constantly broadcasting, to one's own internal ruminations—have a debilitating influence that shows up in everything we think, say, and do.

These are the thoughts that say things like: "Gawd, I'm such a dork for missing that two-footer." "I hate golf, hate life and hate this crappy place," (the scene of your recent quadruple bogey). "Well, I'll probably screw this up really bad, but here goes. . . ." We all have lots of our own bummers we could add to this list.

The point is, it's hard to make pars when thoughts like that are informing our nerves, which inform our muscles, which inform our golf swing.

While our heads are preoccupied in the quagmire of weird thoughts and feelings, our *true voice* gets snuffed out. What is the true voice? Our studies reveal that this is the language of our soul, our "native" voice, the one we were born with. As our training exercises reveal, *our native voice is the one that gives each of us all the right answers always at the right time.* Not just "right" answers, but precisely, minutely perfectly right answers for every question or problem we perceive. Our job is to listen closely and act them out.

Usually our native voice sneaks through only during our infrequent lapses of mental turmoil—then, *sproiiiiing*, our heart wisdom darts into our head or through our body with the perfect idea or solution.

This occurs instantly when we're faced with a problem or have some situation to work out. Even before we get into a mental buzz about it, our native voice is here with the answer, the perfect solution.

Trouble is, we tend not to listen to it. We think we need more complex, convoluted answers, so we let our minds go to work and we become, in a word, hosed. We tend to skip right by our own voice and let the onslaught of second-guessing and mental clamor take us deep into the heart of confusion and conflict.

How many times have you considered your next shot, received a feeling or insight on how to play and which club to use . . . but the mental analysis kicks in and talks you out of your initial intuitive choice. I've lost count of how many times I've heard, usually following a mediocre golf shot, "Well, first I thought I should . . . but then. . . ."

The Law of Spontaneity simply says that when we listen closely for our own inner voice—and remove our attention from the incessant garble of garbage thought patterns that saturate the atmosphere—we can get precisely what we need in any situation.

> In the absence of self-interference—genius.
>
> —FRED SHOEMAKER,
> FOUNDER OF EXTRAORDINARY GOLF

The critical next step, of course, is to acknowledge and act on our true voice. Act on it instantly, spontaneously.

Ever have a ball or club slip out of your hands, but quickly catch it before you even realized what you just did? You didn't have time to think about reaching for it, but the exact right move happened instantly and accurately. Your mind couldn't even begin to figure it out quickly enough, but your native system instantly put every nerve and muscle in exactly the right place. That's one small example of the Law of Spontaneity at work.

This precise response to anything—intuitively, instantly acting without thinking—is always available for everything from game management to hitting golf shots that will make you wonder why you waited so long to trust yourself.

Believe the truth that each of us is born with the ability to know everything we need to accomplish whatever we intend to do, to perfectly meet every challenge we perceive.

All we need do is trust the quiet, powerful voice of our own heart over all others. And be willing to act it out without doubt or hesitation. This willingness triggers an immense array of abilities that have been waiting ages for the call—that is, the trust and belief in oneself—to come forth.

Sure, you'll make a few mistakes as you awaken your sleeping giant within—it may fumble a bit, just as we all do upon arising. But keep trusting your inner voice, your gut feelings, and *keep acting them out*. Soon you'll be most pleasantly surprised at how precisely brilliant you are.

This is literally a "no-brainer"—nothing to figure out. Just listen to yourself and do what comes naturally. And make exactly the right move wherever you are, whatever you're doing.

The Law of Spontaneity holds many gifts and wonderful surprises for sincere students of the game who commit to *being* themselves.

At some point in their evolutions,

even the greatest of masters has stood

right where each of us is right now.

Getting from there to HERE

depends a lot on how much attention

we give our real job: To remember

and act out the truth that we

are perfect, innocent, and worthy

of the best life has to offer.

Law of Acceptance

EACH OF US DESERVES THE FINEST, MOST SATISFYING LIFE—AND GOLF GAME—
POSSIBLE. WHY? BECAUSE WE WERE CREATED AND ARE ALIVE. THAT'S THE ONLY
REQUIREMENT, AND WE ALL MET IT COMING RIGHT OUT OF THE CHUTE.

ONE OF THE most debilitating and degrading influences in our lives and golf games is a self-image many hold, often unknowingly, that we're stranded somewhere between being second-rate wallflowers and quietly desperate fools. Life is a bad joke and we're the stupid punch line. Thinking we're less than perfect is a malady afflicting just about everybody.

Moe Norman (the legendary Canadian golfer who always knows exactly where his clubhead is) and I had one thing in common for a while: We were experts at insuring our own defeat. My self-destructs are too numerous and normal to mention, but some of Moe's are almost surreal. One of his more dramatic demolitions was in the 1971 Quebec Open.

Leading by a stroke, he puts his second shot on the green of the 440-yard 18th hole, the first man to reach it in two that day. But, for some strange reason, the sizeable gallery wasn't applauding his remarkable shot as Moe walked up to the green. Deeply offended, Moe deliberately four-putted as the incredulous gallery watched him throw away the tournament. With each halfhearted swipe of his putter, he reportedly asked his playing partner, "Why didn't they clap?"

Moe seemed more interested in feeling snubbed and martyred than he was in easily winning a golf tournament. As in a Shakespearean tragedy, he played a man seeking respect from others while having none for himself.

But that was then. Moe's unique talents and many accomplishments—in defeat and victory—will inspire and instruct golfers long into the future.

A FRIEND of mine takes a frequent inventory of what she calls the "self-image elements" in her life, golf game and general standing in the world. She talked me into doing this and I found some things I wasn't happy to find, like that for a while I was enjoying being a victim. I somehow had become entranced with playing lousy golf and losing all my change to my accommodating playing partners. "It's a business doing pleasure with you," they'd say all too frequently.

Being a victim was a perversely reassuring place where everything bad that happened could be everyone's responsibility but mine. I could avoid dealing with my life and hide out behind a slapstick golf game.

I hated this feeling, of course, but was afraid to change for fear of having to face up to my choices and be responsible for the life I'd created. So I kept blaming "the world" when it was I who had locked myself in jail.

The only possible "original sin" is the dreary old misconception that there is such a thing.

One thing we can count on: Until we get rid of our guilt and regrets, we keep right on sabotaging ourselves, especially in golf. Until we move beyond the old Puritanic compulsion to punish and degrade ourselves for having made mistakes, we'll be stuck in the "screw me for screwing up" syndrome called the Double Bogey Blues.

Which way outta here? The Law of Acceptance reminds us to:

First, accept what is for what it is—stop wasting time wishing you, people and circumstances were different from what they appear to be. For example, accept your present golf game for what it is here and now—*then* consider what you want to do about it. If you really want to get better, make a serious commitment, stop reacting and start *creating* the game you're dreaming about.

Pay attention and take care of your business regardless of what anyone else thinks, says, or does.

Above all, accept yourself as being just fine the way you are, even though you think you've messed up a lot. You're alive and have an important purpose here. Maybe you're not yet sure what that is, but know that life reveals it to you in many ways.

Clean up your self-image and the world will follow your lead.

Golf, like life in general, gives us pretty much what we believe we deserve.

Meantime, it all comes down to accepting some simple truths:

- We are born innocent.
- We accumulate what appear to be some flaws and unsavory characteristics along the way.
- We hurt others and others hurt us, often unintentionally.
- We feel guilty about our mistakes and often resent others' mistakes.
- We program ourselves with guilt so much that we often punish ourselves—playing golf and other life games like losers—*without even being aware of why we're doing it.*
- We want out of this low-grade condition, but may not quite know how to go about it.

One simple, certain way out of this debilitating loop is a method I know has worked for myself and many others.

Get a notebook and take care of the following:

- List the people that make you feel pain when you think of them.

- Write down each thing they did or didn't do that makes you feel bad.
- After each item, write:
  "I now forgive *myself* for this."
- Make a list of every resentment and regret you're hanging on to.
- After each item, write:
  "I now forgive *myself* for this."

Why forgive *myself*? Sincerely ask yourself this question and you will get your own perfect answer.

Repeat this process once a week, until you have nothing left to write on your list. Naturally, wanting to get your heart and head clear—and stop being a victim—will accelerate this process.

Wonders will occur if you stick with it. A whole new set of positive thoughts and feelings gradually will replace the old self-destruct dæmons we all knew and loved so well. Our real friends and scorecards will be very happy to see them gone.

Acceptance plays a major role in clearing the heart and mind of self-defeating thoughts and feelings, the primary causes of bad golf shots and loss of lunch money.

Get what you truly deserve by forgiving yourself and accepting the truth that you deserve the best!

Cosmic Golf
Training Exercises

THE UNIVERSE GUIDES AND NURTURES

THOSE WHO SINCERELY STRIVE TO UNDERSTAND

AND FOLLOW ITS LAWS.

IT RELENTLESSLY FRUSTRATES, METICULOUSLY

UNRAVELS, AND ULTIMATELY EDUCATES

THOSE WHO DON'T.

(NOTHING PERSONAL.)

WE ARE IMMERSED in a world of miracles, yet seldom pause to wonder about the why and how of them. The following exercises invite you to pause, to look beneath the surface of this amazing world—to look beneath *your* surface—into the miracle of who you really are and all that you can be.

They're primed and waiting to show you how self-knowledge and willingness can make the seemingly impossible come true. They're also a reminder of the awesome powers each of us holds, the dormant infinite knowledge we carry around with us night and day, like forgotten light switches simply waiting to be turned on again.

IMPORTANT NOTE: We begin each exercise with general principles and finish with specific methods by which you can unleash new power and control into your golf game (and other parts of your life as you wish). Each builds on information in the previous one, so by the time you finish you're on a firm foundation and a true roll right into the cup. If you find any exercise too challenging or out of tune with you, just move on to the next one. Take only what feels right.

These exercises are far from the last word on the subject. They're only a brief introduction to a world of endless possibilities for self-recreation. So listen closely for *your own* ideas on how you can use these and other Cosmic Laws to reinvigorate yourself and your golf game.

Loosen up, open up and give these exercises a hearty work-out. They'll show you some stuff you may think you never had—and probably shrink that handicap as well.

So, sandbaggers might as well stop here. Serious golfers, let's go have some fun. . . .

THE WHOLE WORLD IS YOU.

YET YOU KEEP THINKING

THERE IS SOMETHING ELSE.

—Hsüeh-Feng

LIFE IS ETERNAL,

AND THERE IS ONLY

ONE OF US.

—Neale Donald Walsch, *Friendship with God*

You Are Energy *(and it is everywhere)*

ABOUT THIS EXERCISE

COSMIC LAW, LIKE Einstein's Unified Field Theory and many belief systems, invites us to understand that one Source of energy is the life force—and *identity*—of all beings. We're all related because we're extensions of the Source, the Primal One. We even act like relatives sometimes.

Nothing exists outside our true family: people, animals, plants, the natural elements of earth, water, air, fire that compose all physical form including golf balls. Plus, non-physical energies like sound, color, radio, lasers, mental, emotional, spiritual . . . and all the spaces in between.

Even though we've taken different characteristics and appearances, the one Source is our life energy and consciousness. Like drops of water that get involved in any number of odd mixtures, we're still water.

Be what you want the world to be.

—MAHATMA GANDHI

Cosmic law invites us to identify ourselves accurately as the Source, rather than as this little clump of earthen bio-circuitry we call the human body.

When you identify yourself as Source, an inescapable conclusion becomes apparent: The real you is everywhere, the One energy in and around everything. Everything is your body, a highly complex array of tools we created *for the sole purpose of fulfilling our every desire.* Many can't or don't want to believe this, but it's true anyway.

Maybe you're wondering, what's this got to do with my handicap? Only to point out that a fundamental cause of lousy golf is that we tend to relate to the ball and the target as "something else, out there," separate from who we think we are. When it's really a "part of us, right here," inside of us, another kindred drop in the same water hazard of universal energy.

To see anything as being separate from yourself is only a fragmentary human perception, not a fact of life.

It's much easier to accomplish something—like get our finger to scratch our nose, or get the ball in the hole—when we know it's just another part of our body, whose *specifically assigned purpose* is to obey our heart's commands (which it has been doing since our first breath on this planet).

To make use of our universal body, nothing needs to change except the way we see. *We simply change from seeing things as separate from us to seeing them as part of us.* About anything you look at, you can truthfully say, "Hey, that's me, too," and you'd be absolutely right. The universe is your and my body, and all things within it are our cells bouncing along this wild ride through time and space.

All Is One is the first and most important principle of this or any cosmos. Through this truth we take a new integrated look at what used to appear as a chaotic, disintegrated world. We begin to see that we've created our world by our thoughts and feelings about who we are. We begin to see ourselves not as limited little *Homo sapiens* bodies, but as the free, boundless energy that gives life to these bodies and the worlds all around them.

We're the same energy that coalesced to form that tree, that guy over there who just shanked his nine iron, that cloud, those clumps of grass, that jet flying overhead, and everything else in view and in our imagination.

From the beginning, The Primal One has been creating itself through us . . . because *it is us* and all other life visible and invisible.

It's always time to *consciously* express the truth that we're all the same life. In fact, our purpose here is to act out a life that includes everything else as part of who we think we are. *From our identity as Source, we can see and act through everything else, too.*

That's our job. And we might as well include a sterling golf game as part of the deal.

Being the Ball

PURPOSE: To *be* what you want to happen with your golf game.

MATERIALS: Putter and golf ball to start. Rest of the bag later.

DURATION: Ten minutes a day for a few weeks, then constantly.

SETTING: On practice green or other putting surface.

AS MOSES WAS getting ready to head back down the mountain after working out his deal with the burning bush, he asked, "Who shall I say sent me?" The fire in the bush replied, "I Am That I Am. Say this to the people of Israel, I Am sent me to you. . . ." (*Exodus* 3:14)

I Am, the root name for God in many spiritual teachings, is our name, too—because we are one and the same energy. God not only created us, God *is* us and infinitely more.

We speak our real name all the time to create all kinds of things. People usually use *I Am* to recognize existing conditions, such as: "I am sick. I am happy. I am going to make lots of money this year. I am not afraid of this downhill, twelve-foot majorly breaking putt that will win—or lose—me all the skins and presses."

But not so common is the knowledge that when we use the words *I Am* we are actually creating and amplifying the condition by calling in the energy of the most powerful force in the universe, regardless of what title you give it.

The force within this name—God, Primal, Universal Light, whatever you call it—responds in exact proportion to the intensity and awareness of the call. Squeak and you get a little squeak back. Roar like a lion fighting for the life of its mate, and you'll get a somewhat more noticeable response.

A great soul buddy, whom I shall refer to as Het-Bob the One-Putt to protect his questionable reputation and his betting odds, practices the art of seeing himself elsewhere in at least one very practical way. At first he made me promise not to tell anyone his "secret." But when I dangled the possibility of his name appearing in one of the all-time bestselling chartbuster golf books ever written, he started glowing like he'd just dropped a long eagle putt.

Het-Bob's secret is incorporated into this exercise on the simple art of *consciously experiencing yourself as the ball, the cup . . . whatever you want.*

You've heard the expression "Be the ball"? This exercise is here to confirm that *you already are the ball*—all you need to do is act like it! Here we recognize that *"I am* the ball."

The principle involved here works everywhere with everything. For now, though, let's get local and move to the putting green, or your living room carpet, where we can practice not only being everywhere, but making things happen wherever we want.

WE start with a seemingly simple exercise and follow with a more challenging one. Don't be concerned if these seem a little south of normal. It may help to pretend you're at a party and your host (me) proposes a crazy new game. Just play along for a while and have some fun with this.

FOR THE BEGINNING STUDENT
THE HET-BOB FACTOR:

1) Place a golf ball twelve feet from the cup, or a glass on its side on your carpet. Set up for a putt as you normally would. Now stroke the ball to the hole.
2) Now pretend you are the cup down there, vigorously inhaling like a strong vacuum, so that when the ball comes near it will be sucked in. (On the golf course, you'll want to do this quietly—but let 'er rip for now!)

Inhale loudly so the air rushing into the cup sounds like the roaring whir of your real vacuum cleaner as it glides across the rug. *Feel* the ball being irresistibly pulled into the cup.

YOU laugh! But I have seen many of Het-Bob's and my own close putts pulled *sideways* into the cup.

I suspect Het-Bob was led to this secret by years of study and intense practice in the art of French kissing. The same principle is at work in golf—see the footnote on the next page.

FOR THE ADVANCED STUDENT

1) Place a golf ball twelve feet from the cup, or a glass on its side on your carpet. Even though it may sound crazy at first, say to yourself at least three times: "I am the mascu-

line ball. I am the feminine cup.* I am the green lying all around us." As best you can, believe what you're saying (because it's true).

2) Imagine actually being the golf ball, looking back up at your body as you repeat a few more times, "I am the masculine ball." Get your awareness right down there and feel your rubbery innards and texture of the dimples that cover your skin. Feel the stirring in your very core as you yearn to unite with the feminine cup. Do you see your human head up there talking away?

   Notice how you can focus and observe your self-awareness anywhere you like.

3) Now move your attention to the cup, and repeat the above process. See yourself as the cup as you say a few times, "I am the feminine cup." Visualize it as best you can. Ooh, it's warm and inviting in here! Look up out of you-the-cup, over toward where you-the-ball lies, and up to where you-the-face is looking down at you.

   Feel the attraction between your ball and your cup selves growing stronger, getting warmer. With great passion, both of you say, "I want you *now!*"

4) Feeling a tremendous surge of magnetic attraction growing between your ball and your cup, set up to the ball and stroke it toward the hole. As you do, picture

---

*We'll be working with balls and cups a lot in these exercises. This is natural, of course: The nature of a cup is to be filled. By its design, a cup actually *wants* to be filled—like the soil wants to be filled with seeds, like a woman wants to be filled with a man. A ball actually *wants* to go in the cup—like a seed wants to enter the soil, like a man wants to enter a woman.

The ball is Alpha. The cup is Omega. And they're in love! So there's a certain amount of natural magnetic attraction already helping the ball and cup fulfill their destiny. This exercise is here only to help that process along.

yourself again as the ball, now driving breathlessly toward the cup like an ardent suitor bearing a bouquet of roses to his sweetheart. You're the ball, the main dude, and you got a date.

Picture you-the-cup here in the doorway, gasping deeply as you see this big guy heading your way. He's cool and he's got what you want, and you got what he wants. You reach out and pull him into your outstretched arms. Now the both of you are swept by a deliciously irresistible force that compels you to melt into the oneness of your destiny.

You'll recognize this re-union by that soft rattle a ball makes as it plunges into the heart of the cup.

Note: Players with heart problems should consider using a more toned-down version of this exercise.

Practice this and soon it will become more natural feeling. Let yourself *feel* the primal forces of nature that compel your manly ball and womanly cup to merge in happy re-union. Yes, seeing yourself as both ball and cup at once is a stretch. So *stretch* and see what happens!

This is perfectly in accord with similar re-unions that occur night and day throughout nature. Masculine-feminine polarity is universal, so why shouldn't it be perfectly natural here? Believe me, this will be routine stuff in a short time, once you get past how weird it seems at first.

Okay, okay, okay! For many, this exercise will invoke natural skepticism and even a few horse laughs. But don't let it stop you from giving it a good honest workout. You may find the laughs turning into hoots of amazement!

Please don't go through this routine on the golf course—do it at home or on the practice range. When you go golfing, just take the *experience* of the exercise with you. Remember the feeling of the powerful attraction between ball and cup as you step up to each shot. Just feel it as a natural force at work, not as a bunch of mental details.

The larger purposes here are to re-train one's awareness to include:

- everything outside your biochemical earth-clump body, to see the rest of the world as being yourself,
- acting through your greater self,
- the forces of nature and the powerful magnetic attraction that cause polar opposites to re-unite, and
- revolutionary new ways to find love in your golf game.

The principle involved often is erroneously referred to as "projection," which we engage in all the time, often unknowingly, by the thoughts we direct at others. But that's an inaccurate term to use here. We're simply practicing the truth of who we are as Source energy, *already everywhere and everything*—so there's no "other" to project ourselves onto.

We're practicing not only an awareness that includes the rest of our known world, but *how to act through these other parts of our newly discovered body*. Not only being the ball, but *doing things as the ball*. There's the rub indeed.

The Laws of Polarity and Attractions can be lots of fun if you're willing to party with them. Make no mistake, they're ready to rock anytime you are.

IMAGINATION (IMAGE-IN-ACTION) IS THE TOOL

WE HAVE USED ALL ALONG — OFTEN UNCONSCIOUSLY —

TO CREATE OUR GOLF GAMES

AND THE REST OF OUR WORLD.

BEFORE WE CAN USE IMAGINATION CONSCIOUSLY

AND TO ITS FULLEST POWER,

WE MUST FIRST LEARN TO CLEAR OUR MINDS

AND BE STILL.

Being Still

A QUIET HEART OPENS THE GATES
AND LETS OUR ANGELS IN TO PLAY

ABOUT THIS EXERCISE

A PRIMARY FUNCTION of truth is to drive us out of our logical mind—are we here yet?—and into the world of intuition or soul. (Note: being "out of your mind" is not to be confused with insanity, which implies a debilitated mind.)

Truth returns us to a world of wonders and limitless possibilities we all knew as children. A time before our golf games got lost in ruminations, fears, worries, doubts, limits, conditionings, reactions, and stress that unfortunately describe the "normal" world of the typical human mind. All of these nagging energies *have no choice* but to show up in our golf games and the rest of our lives. They're energy seeds whose nature is to grow as long as we permit them to remain planted in our bio-systems.

So how do we return from there (the land of dog-eat-dog) to here (the land of miracles)? Television, the great global hypnotizer, offers some important clues. You flop down on the couch, turn on your television set and select a favorite program. Unless you have transmission or equipment problems, everything comes in nice and clear.

The mind is like a garden. Naturally, before we can plant our chosen seeds in it, we first cultivate the soil and clear out the weeds.

Now picture your mind as a television set (in a way, it really is). All the thoughts hanging around and passing through your mind are the programs being aired. Now quickly review what thoughts are showing in your mind today, the recurring programs appearing on your inner TV set.

First, are you aware that *these programs are only thoughts that you can accept or reject at will?* Can you change your mind's channels (thoughts) whenever you want? Can you tune in any program and watch it as long as you like? Can you create your own programs? Can you turn the set off? What's it like when your inner set is turned off?

What remains when no programs are showing, when no thoughts are present?

What's left is you. Your plain ol' self—without all the "pro-gramming" of distractions and reactions buzzing through your brain. Just you. The presence of consciousness without all the clutter. This is what Zen refers to as "mindlessness." It doesn't mean you're lost, although it might feel that way without all the familiar noises and images that usually pack our heads.

It means you're found. You've finally found yourself as free energy, the real you—a ray of Primal One, the Source.

When you are still for even a few moments, your perception of yourself as just a little human being gently diffuses into the form-less silence, into what Shivas Irons describes in *Golf in the Kingdom* as the Fertile Void—the native soil out of which we create our-selves. This is Primal's playing field, where everything is possible.

The real you, Source, uses a very real language you can study and regain fluency in. It's our native voice speaking in our ancient native tongue—one we all used to know very well, but have mostly forgotten over the long haul of history.

Source is always right here waiting to be heard when all the noise is switched off and our inner screen is clear. *Source agreed not to assert itself into our human free will—so it waits 'til we choose it over all the other options.*

To choose our Source option, we first have to acknowledge that it exists. Then we need to be still so it can operate free from the mind's nagging, fretting self-defeat mechanisms.

While the mind is handy for computing mundane affairs (taxes, grocery lists, box scores), it's also filled with gobs of debilitating programs we've allowed to impede our growth and success.

To be still is to listen only to our own Source presence and native thoughts, the ones designed to make our finest dreams come true. (Also see *Who's Calling Your Shots?*)

Clearing the Screen

PURPOSE: To quiet the mind so your dream golf shots have a clear path to realization.

MATERIALS: A shag bag full of willingness to relax and let go for a while.

DURATION: Thirty days, ten to fifteen minutes a day. Constantly after that.

SETTING: A quiet place anywhere. Later, everywhere you are.

BEING STILL IS when all the mental dogs have stopped barking and whining . . . and the only one present is pure, powerful, peaceful you. Some people think, in their frantic world of tumult and shouting, that such a place would be boring with nothing to do. Yet this is the seeding ground where you create your entire world.

Here's how you can experience this for yourself.

Being still for ten to fifteen minutes each day allows at least three vitally important accomplishments:

1) Enjoy a welcome rest from all the noisy, pestering, debilitating thought patterns that constantly bombard the human mind.

2) Get better acquainted with your Source Self, the real you

that exists before, during, and after all the mental movies stop running.

3) Learn to operate free of those dozen or so conflicting anxiety-riddled swing thoughts that jam your head starting with your setup and continuing through the golf ball flying on its way to wherever.

MANY people clear their screens through meditation, a practice that means something a bit different to everybody. Meditation simply is a way to quiet the mind and thus become aware of our real identity as pure, free energy beings. It's a way to recognize and invite our Source Self to come on in and take charge of our whole operation.

Meditation—being still—gives our Source Self the opportunity to re-order our human energy patterns and plant the seeds of satisfaction deep into our consciousness *where they begin to re-create our world in their image*. The new seeds immediately begin to replace less satisfying ones we've been letting in since long ago.

Being still tremendously accelerates this process by clearing away old thought patterns that keep us stuck in our old mud. Our Source power can't do very much if we block it out with a tense, noisy head jammed full of anxieties and ruminations. How can you dance in a room stacked high with years of accumulated mental sludge and junk piles?

So when we are still, even for a few minutes, our soul can shine right in and start partying with our cells.

A sit-down meditation is an excellent way to *experience* what it's like to be pure, unencumbered energy.

Don't shy away from this silent encounter with your native self. Let curiosity win out over reluctance and resistance. Open to your own vast universe that's been waiting only for your permission to show you the huge awesome being you really are.

As you practice and get better at being still, you can learn to enter this meditative state of being on the golf course or wherever you happen to be. Then you can clear your screen, call up the swing thoughts you want to appear and know that no other thought energy can interfere with you now.

HERE'S an all-purpose exercise in learning to be still—to keep your golf swing free from shank-causing mental cacophony. So your true intentions can have center stage and carry out your visions of greatness from tee to green . . . and at the bar where they're shoveling greenbacks at you.

Use the following suggestions as a guide to develop your own meditation system. Above all, keep it simple and humble. Don't use this practice like it's a 900-number psychic hotline.

Soon you'll be standing over the ball, free of negative influences, with only your intentions all lined up to bring out the best you got.

1) Pick a time every day that's convenient for

you. Make it something regular you do—like morning coffee or tea—not something you'll do if you get around to it.

2) As you sit, check the time and say something like, "I have nothing to do but be still for the next ten (or fifteen or thirty) minutes, so I don't need to be anxious about getting going. *I'll do all that when I'm finished.*"

3) Take some nice deep, slow breaths to settle down. Then ask your version of your own higher power—God, Source, Higher Self, Soul, whatever fits you—to take charge of this time and bring forth its perfection through you now.

   Now imagine a brilliant sun shining in the center of your chest. After a moment, let it expand to fill the entire room. See your body sitting in the middle of this sun now.

4) If thoughts come bothering you, say, "It's just a thought," and let it go. As you identify it as just a thought, it loses its power to interfere with you. Keep identifying thoughts that come, and keep returning your attention to the sun image you're focusing on.

   The more you focus on your sun, the less you'll notice other things.

5) Now just be still and enjoy this sun bath for a while. Know ahead of time that your busy little mind will want to comment on everything and bring in all kinds of thoughts to distract you. Keep identifying them as "just thoughts" and keep returning to your sun.

6) Don't micromanage this operation! Just be quiet and let your Higher Self have you for a while. You may experience some sensations or nothing at all. It doesn't matter.

What matters is that you surrender to your Self all con-
cerns about what's going on.

*Have faith that the greatest blessings possible for you at this time
are being instilled in your consciousness.*

7) When you end the meditation, you can wrap it up with a
   little thanks if you like. Now's a good time to "place your
   order" (see *Law of Intentions*).

Some also find an affirmation helpful, such as, "I walk this
day in peace and truth for the good of all," or "I'm going to grip
it and rip it 'til my hands bleed." Say whatever positive thought
or impulse occurs to you.

The object here is to learn the language of your heart,
Source's operations center. It will tell you everything you need
to know all the time, in a variety of ways—through your intuition, ideas, other people, circumstances and conditions, on the
street and on the golf course.

Everywhere your heart is talking to you. Be still, listen, and
you'll hear it. It's always present with perfect guidance and solutions to every situation you create or encounter on the golf
course and everywhere else.

Some days "being still" may be noisy and tough to focus.
Other days it'll be easier. The key is to do it regularly so it can
become a part of your daily routine. As you learn to listen and
absorb your own higher wisdom during these meditation peri-
ods, you'll be much more able to do it during your golf game.

Your Source would love to give you a perfect golf shot every
time. While your human mind is full of programs that want to
see your clubs flying into the nearest water hazard chased by
your vows to quit this blasted game forever.

Which would you rather have in charge of your clubhead, and your other head as well?

Practicing meditation on a regular basis can release immense new power for you to naturally dissolve old self-destruct patterns and replace them with the golf shots you've been dreaming of. (Also see related exercise, *Holes in Your Head*.)

So consider making a practice of Being Still every day.*

A major shift will occur when you can clear your screen, produce your own programs for a successful golf game, and play them on your inner television set. Then enjoy watching your fine new shot-making show as it plays out on the golf course.

This exercise may take a lifetime to perfect, but it will yield many extraordinary gifts along the way. It will gradually explain the new saying, "Being here is all the fun."

---

*I heartily recommend another excellent meditation idea that begins on p. 200 of *Friendship with God* (hardcover) by Neale Donald Walsch. Don't be surprised if you find yourself irresistibly drawn into the rest of this beautiful book.

THINKING IS THE HARDEST WORK THERE IS,

WHICH IS THE PROBABLE REASON SO FEW ENGAGE IN IT.

—Henry Ford

Who's Calling Your Shots?

ATTENTION LIKE WATER, MIND LIKE HOSE—
WHERE YOU POINT IT, SOMETHING GROWS.

ABOUT THIS EXERCISE

REAL THINKING IS hard, as Mr. Ford notes, mainly because it requires sustained, purposeful concentration—while most of us find it much easier to kick back and let the mind run rampant as it will.

Most of what passes for thinking would more accurately be called ruminating, worrying, fretting, fuming, grinding. In other words, most "thinking" that occurs actually is negative reacting and mental jabbering. Real thinking is creating, using one's heart to conceive, to invent, to imagine.

This exercise is about learning to take creative control of your thought world, and thus the life it creates, by: 1) Removing destructive thoughts, and 2) Nurturing constructive ones.

You can trace every lousy golf shot directly back to an equally lousy thought. If you don't believe me, just ask this old saying: "Every action that ever occurred was first given birth by its parent thought." While that may seem obvious at first glance, it may be worth a closer look. Ever wonder where these lousy thoughts come from? Or why you're "thinking" them in the first place?

If *thoughts* are the parents, then *actions* are their kids. By its nature, every thought is like a momma bird, always looking for a place to hatch and nurture her young in someone's mind. Quick quiz: What kind of thought eggs are hatching in your nest today?

The mind is an incubator for an infinite variety of migrant thoughts, all wanting to have children (expression) through us. For most of us, our mind is like a zoo where some thought birds flit in and out every few seconds, while others may hang around for years. Some we latch on to and feed with our attention, which is the baby food that makes thoughts grow big and strong. Some loiter around in the back rooms, never really coming or going, energy fluffs too coagulated to evaporate, too undernourished to fully manifest.

Diverse as it is, the whole menagerie of our mental zoo can fit into two distinct categories:

NATIVE THOUGHTS. These carry our essential operating instructions that come with the package when we're born. They spring from the soul, blossom into the mind, and provide us with a natural flow of ideas and information *specifically designed to help us fulfill our life's purpose.*

Because it's their nature, they're always positive, inspiring, uplifting, here to help us succeed. They're our natural children, hungry for nurturing so they can grow up and help us lead fulfilling, satisfying lives.

Each person has his own deep well of uniquely formulated native thoughts, yet they're often buried under the noise and pandemonium that usually fill our minds. But they're always trying to work their way out into our world where they naturally belong. Their sole purpose is to manifest happiness and success.

When we let them come out and play—and don't bury them in doubt and mental clamor—they do just that.

MASS THOUGHTS. These come from the dumping ground of thoughts and feelings that people are continuously broadcasting into the planetary atmosphere. Like formless energy wave-clumps, they hover and waft about, looking for people to let them in so they can enter the physical world.

And we—like the radio receivers/transmitters we are—often unconsciously allow these mass leftovers to enter our bio-systems and act through us to fulfill their random purposes.

Mass thoughts live off our life energy like parasites, distracting us from our real purpose here, which is *to give life to our soul's visions and ideas.*

These mental migrants are best ignored or tossed in the fire (later in this exercise). While some mass thoughts may seem helpful, most are negative or inappropriate because they're designed for someone else, not you. They're like toothbrushes or underwear, personal things you wouldn't usually borrow from others.

When we feel afraid, feel stupid and worthless, or criticize and condemn ourselves and others . . . it's not really "I" (our native thought) speaking. It's those random mass thoughts hatching their weird, self-defeating offspring into our world.

So we have two types of thoughts—native and mass—that give us two ways of seeing the world within and around us. You can tell which ones are having their way with you by noting their characteristics:

Native thoughts arise naturally when our hearts and minds are clear, when we're conscious, alert, acting and feeling in harmony with ourselves. They create positive actions. They gather vital energy around us.

Mass thoughts create a negative state of mind, often instilling bad feelings about ourselves and others. They create negative reactions. They drain and dissipate our vital energy.

Would it be a good idea to know which thoughts are your own native helpers and which are vagrant energy burglars that just want to lunch on your life energy and don't really care what happens to you?

Here's a way to sort them out, get rid of the carpetbaggers, and put the good guys to use hitting great golf shots, or anything else you want to do with them.

- If you're a "note taker" type, keep a little notebook around. If not, keep track of the following in your head. Make two headings: one for "Native Thoughts" and one for "Mass Thoughts."
- As you breeze through the day and relax into the evening,

pause now and then and jot a quick word or phrase noting the predominant thoughts that keep reappearing in your mind. Decide which heading each thought should go under. A key word or two will do.

- Every day, conduct a brief "Thought Inventory." Identify each one as just an idea knocking at your mind's door—*not* as something "you think" or "you are." Distinguish between your "native" helpers and the "mass" meanderers.

Simply identifying these thoughts is a major step toward getting free of those you don't want. Keep reminding yourself: "These thoughts *aren't me*. They're just options I can choose or reject at will."

You'll soon notice how mass thoughts tend to weaken and distract you. And how your own native thoughts give you power and confidence. How many of each kind are acting through your body right now?

You alone have the power to decide what hangs around in your mind. Picture your mind as your home—it truly is!—and see thoughts as visitors at the door. Who are you going to let in when they come knocking? What unwanted ne'er-do-wells are you going to turn back out to the streets or heave into the fire?

Our mental home deserves at least as much respect and care as the house we live in!

The following exercise offers a simple yet very powerful means to get rid of what you don't want in your mind and golf game—and bring forth your own native plan for success and satisfaction.

Black Ball/White Ball

PURPOSE: To eliminate negative thoughts that cause lousy golf shots, and replace them with ones that create good golf shots.

MATERIALS: Paper or mental notepad, and an average imagination.

DURATION: Do this for two to three weeks and note results.

SETTING: Wherever you happen to be.

BLACK BALL

TO GET RID of negative thoughts that keep appearing on your list (or in your mind as you're standing over your golf ball), here's a fun and very effective way to do it:

1) Tally up the mass thoughts you don't want in your life anymore, or just one or two that are currently bugging you. Now be still a moment and close your eyes. With your imagination, visualize a black golf ball sitting on a green about six inches from the cup.

2) Next, look down into the cup and imagine the inside of it blazing with blue-white hot fire, like you see with a high-octane blowtorch. This fire spreads out below the cup to an area the size of the earth, so don't worry about overloading it.

3) Now pour your unwanted thoughts into the black ball, which immediately absorbs them. Then tap it into the fiery hole and watch it vaporize *instantly*!

As you do this, say something like: "Adios, ol' buddies, you don't live here anymore. Go back to where you came from." Be sure they stay gone by never giving them even an erg of attention ever again.

You may need to do this a few times to permanently get rid of some persistent, long-standing negative thoughts. But hey, it's just a tap in! You can't miss.

In all seriousness, strange as it may seem, this exercise has the power to really clear the mental airwaves so your positive native thoughts can take their rightful place and start making your finest imaginings and swing dreams come true.

Thoughts R *not* Us

WHITE BALL

TO REINFORCE your native thoughts, use a similar method as follows:

1) Imagine a white ball sitting six inches from the cup. Pour whatever ideals and primo swing images you want into this white ball.

2) Now imagine the bottom of the cup as a window to a sparkling blue sky filled with the most dazzling sunlight you've ever seen. This is your infinite storehouse of everything you value and want to be in your life.

   When you drop something into this sky, it becomes an energized starseed nurturing your ideals for as long as you want them to be.

3) Load up the white ball and tap it into the sunlight cup. As you do this, say something like: "This is what I want to be and *I accept that it will happen* continuously in my life."

These exercises truly work! You can prove it to yourself anytime you really want to.

As you relieve yourself of foreign, negative thoughts and let your own native voice be heard, you'll feel yourself coming more alive, doing things better with less effort. Playing the game with much more satisfaction. Sinking more putts!

By the thoughts we choose to allow in our hearts, we thereby choose the kind of life we experience. We always, always have a choice.

You'll be burning up all those voices—some who've dogged you for years—telling you that you can't realize the best of who you are, filling you with self-defeating excuses and doubts that make you blow shots and gouge away at your game.

When they're pretty much gone, what's left? Just your naturally perfect self ready to do some naturally miraculous stuff wherever you are.

Be the White Ball and see what happens. . . .

A FIRM DECISION CREATES A POWERFUL INNER MAGNET

THAT LITERALLY ATTRACTS EVERYTHING

NECESSARY TO REALIZE ITSELF.

THIS MAGNET ALSO BECOMES AN IMPENETRABLE

ELECTROMAGNETIC SHIELD THAT DEFLECTS

ANY DETRIMENTAL INFLUENCES.

Believe and It's Yours

BELIEF IS THE BRIDGE THAT TAKES
US FROM HOPING TO *KNOWING*.

ABOUT THIS EXERCISE

YOU'RE INVITED TO join the growing number of dropouts from the Pavlovian School of Conditioned Disasters, and enroll in the University of Yourself.

The purpose of this exercise is to rebuild confidence in our own ability to create—from within our deep well of native power—the golf game and anything else we desire. This is one of the most fundamental and quickly satisfying classes at U of Y.

We all have the power and ability to consciously direct ourselves as we wish—especially after we rid ourselves of debilitating thought patterns (as in *Who's Calling Your Shots?* above).

Start small at first—small decisions, small victories—so you can easily demonstrate the truth of these principles for yourself. You'll soon find many uses for this exercise to help you do things you thought were never possible, like get your ball into the cup with noticeably fewer strokes.

I use this simple yet illuminating exercise many different ways to instill some effortless magic into all the games I play. It's "effortless" because you program yourself with a firm intention (place your order), agree and insist that it occur—then stop thinking about it. Your intention magnet does all the work. Let it be and let it happen.

This exercise holds a lifetime of endless possibilities for golf and everything else. What follows is just a little peek into the promised land of conscious self-creation. Where you go with it from here, of course, is up to you.

Some years ago, I taught this exercise to my then-twelve-year-old son, who has become quite adept at it and puts it to many beneficial uses. I *know* it works, and you will, too.

FAITH IS NOT JUST A WISHFUL HOPE FOR THE BETTER,

BUT A POWERFUL, ACTIVE FORCE THAT SURROUNDS

AND GOES BEFORE US TO MANIFEST

THE OBJECT OF OUR FAITH.

IT IS THE PRIMARY TOOL OF SELF-MASTERY.

Wake-up Call

PURPOSE: To teach yourself how to do, with certainty, whatever you want.

MATERIALS: A strong inner voice that commands and accepts no excuses.

DURATION: Four-week proof period. Then, probably forever.

SETTING: In your bed (or any bed) just before you go to sleep.

1) Each night in bed just before you check out, decide what time you want to wake up in the morning. Don't set your regular alarm clock. Instead, set your "inner" clock. Say this to yourself: "I intend to have a good night's rest, and wake up refreshed and feeling fine. I intend to awaken at precisely 6:15 A.M. (or whenever you like). I *will* wake up at 6:15 A.M."

   Firmly plant the command seed in the awaiting soil of your mind. Remember: It's your mind's job to carry out your instructions, not vice versa.

2) Be alert to detect any mass thought intruders that say you can't, won't or shouldn't wake up at precisely 6:15 A.M. As you note any such thoughts, *quickly* bundle them up into the Black Ball and tap them into the fiery cup, as in the previous exercise.

Allow no excuses for failure. You're going to do this—period. No back-door bailouts. You have irrevocably decided and that's it. You want an excuse to whine and complain? Find it somewhere else. *This* is going to work!

3) For a few moments, you may want to review the day's activities, see where you did well and note where you could do better. Then forgive all that needs forgiving and lay it all down so you don't drag today's divots into tomorrow.

Now repeat your decision and intent: "I will awaken at precisely 6:15 A.M." Briefly envision yourself waking up in the morning and seeing the clock hands standing right at 6:15 A.M.

Don't ruminate about how this is going to happen or you'll undermine your decision. As you drift off to sleep, think only about things you like, things that make you feel good. And be ready to wake up at precisely 6:15 A.M.

Do this every night you can for a month, and you will see for yourself that this exercise really works. Practice first on days when your wake-up time won't endanger your job. Allow some time to get confidence in this.

The first few days you may (or may not!) sleep past your intended time—but that's okay. Give it a fair chance. Keep practicing and be willing to let it happen. That is, don't secretly tell yourself it won't work. Secretly tell yourself it *will* and you'll be most pleasantly surprised. *It will work precisely as much as you believe it will.* Believe and it's yours!

EXERCISE NOTES: Persevere with this exercise, and in a surprisingly short time you will be waking up exactly when you have declared you will. Give this the same amount of time you spent learning how to type or ride a bike—its potential for personal re-creation is infinitely more valuable! Soon you'll be well on your way, ready to demonstrate these newly refined abilities on the golf course.

ON THE GOLF COURSE

HOW MANY WAYS can you think of to apply this exercise on the golf course? Well, how many decisions do you make during a round of golf?

As you consider each shot, determine exactly what you want and declare your firm intention to have it be so. Command and accept that it will happen. Then let it go, and swing away with the faith that you'll get what you intend to be.

How many times has your focus been fuzzy and you approach a shot with only a rough idea of what you want? You know it: Rough idea = rough shot. Precise intention = precise result much more probable.

How many times have you feared that something would go wrong somewhere between your setup and your ball coming to rest out there somewhere? As you're lining up each shot, absolutely zap that little niggling voice that's telling you that you can't pull this off. Quickly use the Black Ball exercise if necessary—do this in one or two seconds at most.

Visualize the exact shot you want—and *agree that it will occur.* Not that it can occur. Insist and accept that it WILL occur. Why should you accept anything less? *Why?*

Got any more self-defeating excuses to get rid of? Do it now, quickly, and move on!

To make this work, one must assume the right attitude: You're not on your hands and knees here groveling and hoping. You're *commanding* and accepting nothing less than your ideal results. Recognize no limits or excuses for failure.

Naturally, you may not get 100% results for a while, or maybe even for a long time. Then again, maybe you will. Just don't think you've failed if you don't hit a home run every time. Even the best, highest paid baseball players are happy to bat .300 or so. If we amateurs can start off with one for four or better, that's real progress.

Just for perspective, remember that many of us are rejuvenating our attitudes from a long history of self-defeat and dogging frustration, especially in golf. You usually don't get rid of deeply imbedded conditioning overnight—but we can do it a little bit at a time. *We are doing it right now. And we'll keep on doing it 'til we bat 1.000.*

It may take some time to get used to the fact that we truly can have what we want if we demand and *accept* it. So stick with it! Actually, we have no choice. It's a matter of when, not if, because it's the job we came here to do.

At the very least, you will begin to see a marked increase in accuracy and the satisfaction only a fine golf shot can bring. At the most, well, your sparkling blue sky's the limit. . . .

He attempts nothing and all things are accomplished.

He is silent and his voice is heard everywhere.

He forgets himself and remembers everything.

Thus does the superior man fulfill his destiny.

—Lao Tzu

The Magic Triangle

ABOUT THIS EXERCISE

WHEN I WAS attending U.S. Army Airborne School at Fort Benning, Georgia, I met a pistol expert named Jake who unknowingly gave me a profound insight into the mysteries of golf. I'd left my clubs behind when I entered military service, but Jake's incredible teaching later produced amazing results not only in my golf game, but in many other activities as well.

Jake recently had completed an unusual training course in shooting handguns. His instruction had been just the opposite of the traditional mechanical approach familiar to most of us:

Bring the pistol out front to shoulder height, aim down the sight as you bring it in line with the target, breathe out slowly and gently squeeze the trigger—or variations on that scenario.

Jake told me about a radical new way he'd just learned the art of highly consistent, accurate pistol shooting:

"Our small class was made up of average guys and no one was a skilled marksman," Jake said. "In fact, we'd been picked because we'd shown little talent with firearms. The first thing we were told was to forget everything we'd ever learned or thought we knew about using handguns, or any guns.

"Our instructor, an army sergeant, then described the concept of developing automatic, precision hand-eye-target coordination. A perfect triangle formed by the imaginary lines connecting our hand, eye, and target, he told us, automatically creates itself—and consequently a perfect shot—when we learn to let it happen.

"It's a Magic Triangle that always naturally occurs when our eye locks on a target. But we tend to prevent it when we turn this triangle into a straight, rigid line by 'taking aim' as we'd always been taught.

"The Sarge went on to say that we needed to accept the fact that we are naturally supposed to hit the target—every single time. 'Why shouldn't you?' he asked us one day. 'You keep thinking how difficult it is and that you're likely to miss, when you should be thinking that the most natural thing in the world is for you to hit the target exactly where you're looking at it. So stop messing with the shot. Stop *thinking* and do it.'

"Sarge told us that the only thing we were to keep in mind, to visualize, is the shot hitting the target. We were not to aim in any way, or even look at our pistols. We were to focus total-y on the target and 'let' our natural hand-eye-target coordination bring the pistol into perfect position with no mental tampering on our part.

"Then he started us shooting BB pistols—every shot at a different target. We could easily see where the BBs were hitting. After watching hundreds of BBs going every which way, our subconscious systems automatically began to align our shooting hands with the target. Look and fire. Soon we started hearing the satisfying sound of BBs pinging off our random targets.

"'Never the same target,' Sarge kept telling us, 'because that leads to mechanical conditioning, and our purpose here is to de-condition you, unbind you from your mental gridlock. When you see a target I want you fluid, flexible, spontaneous, non-thinking, purely responding to what your eyes see, instantly flowing into a perfect hand-eye-target triangle.

"'You can't do that when you're trying to aim the weapon. Trying is the worst thing you can do! *Trying keeps you from doing.*'

"At first I didn't quite grasp what he was saying. How can you do something without trying? But we kept practicing this way every day. It amazed me how much my reflexes kept wanting to 'aim' the pistol. And doubts always came up about how I could hit something without aiming at it. But after a while the instruction really started kicking in.

"We moved from BB pistols to .22 semi-automatics, with increasingly accurate results. I quit trying so hard and found myself 'doing' it simply by focusing on the target and letting my hand swing up and fire without thinking or aiming. Pretty soon we were shooting cans out of the air. Some shooters were nailing small paper plates and even coins tossed in the air.

"Instantly hitting whatever I was looking at became second

nature, simple and natural. I didn't think about trying to do it.
I just did it.

"I began to feel an amazing sense of power and confidence,
like I'd been let in on some very secret knowledge. This was too
easy! It wasn't until later that I began to understand the profound nature of that instruction. Ol' Sarge was a lot more than
some guy with a few stripes on his sleeves."

I never saw Jake again, but his story ignited a fire in me. I
hadn't realized it at the time, but Jake had confirmed a method
ol' Arjuna had used to nail the eye of the fish (see first section,
"Inside the Kingdom").

He was describing the timeless laws: You "become" or attain
exactly what you focus your attention on. The more precise and
concentrated your focus, the more precise the result. Only mental distraction and doubt can prevent it from happening.

Natural perfection always happens—*is supposed to happen*—
when you completely trust and allow it. However you say it,
the fundamental truth is the same.

Through the years and in many different ways I've practiced
the Magic Triangle—practiced *doing-not-trying*—in spite of my
stubborn, jabbering, micromanaging mind. I've seen amazing
results of this exercise in myself and in others.

Once at a friend's country place, I picked up a bow and
arrow for the first time in fifteen years. The target was a square
of insulation board strung between two trees about fifty feet
away. It had a bull's-eye painted on it and at the center was a
hole clean through the board about one inch in diameter.

I strung the arrow, lasered my eye on the target, and quickly visualized it flying through the hole. As I did this, Jake's
story, thoughts of Arjuna, and *Zen in the Art of Archery* wafted

through my mind. Then, just as I cleared my mental screen, the arrow released and I watched it zip through that hole and stick in a far tree.

I handed the bow back to my unbelieving friend. He wanted me to do it again to prove it wasn't just luck. "Not again," I said, "I already did that one. This is about every spontaneous new shot *now*—not trying to repeat something you just did."

I've done the same thing with slingshots, rocks, star knives, spitballs and golf balls. *The Magic Triangle principle applies to anything you use to connect with any kind of target.*

Even such glimpses are enough to confirm that this principle is real and does work. Of course, some days are better than others, and it takes perseverance to prove these principles day in and day out. But when you demonstrate your own proof, *you'll know.*

These skills lie dormant in every living being. Remember, the only prerequisite for success is that you were born.

At home and office, walking around outside, on the driving range and putting green, in our mind, on the golf course . . . everywhere we can practice the Magic Triangle. Use any opportunity anywhere, anytime to sharpen your eye-hand-target coordination. Effects of this fun practice will show up in your golf game, too.

Always a Different Target

PURPOSE: To learn the Magic Triangle and get it working for you.
MATERIALS: Anything handy, including golf balls.
DURATION: One month random practice. Then, probably forever.
SETTING: Anywhere you are, on or off the golf course.

HERE ARE A few ways to refine your use of the Magic Triangle at home, work or play. You can probably think of many others that will work just as well. And remember, for best results, stay loose and have fun with these.

BASIC GUIDES FOR THIS EXERCISE:

- Focus your attention only on connecting with the target—nothing else.
- Your eye instantly receives all essential information with which you automatically program your system to make its connection.
- Always a different target, or different position from same target.
- Don't aim in any way or try to consciously control your shot.

- Expect a little resistance and be willing to miss a lot as your body and mind adapt to this new skill.
- Relax and trust yourself. Let go and see what happens.

AT HOME, AT WORK

USE WADS of paper, wiffle golf balls, or whatever's handy. Throw them at random targets, abiding by the above rules. Be aware of the automatically occurring triangle formed by the lines connecting your eye, hand (object you're throwing) and target.

Be sure to pick up after yourself so the local authorities don't get after you.

OUT WALKING AROUND

HERE'S WHERE you can really get some practice in by throwing rocks, sticks, using sling shots, bow and arrow, handguns (like Jake). Anything you use in accordance with the above rules surely will refine your hand-eye-target coordination. And that will naturally rub off on your golf game, especially the short game and putting.

AT THE DRIVING RANGE

WARM UP AND do your normal range routine for ten minutes or so. Then start picking random targets—remember, always a different one—at various distances: flags or markers, other range balls, terrain features such as bumps or depressions, light and dark spots. Hit five or six shots with each club and try to use all your clubs before you finish.

Don't be concerned about actually hitting the target at first. If you do, that's great, but no biggie if you don't right away. Simply focus on seeing the hand-eye-target triangle happen *without any effort*. Let the results start showing up on their own time. They won't take that long, depending on how

Mechanical, repetitive practice is like a pianist playing musical scales to learn and refine technique. Using the Magic Triangle is like a pianist playing a totally unique live concert, unrepeatable, perfectly realizing the highest potential of each moment.

much you're willing to let go of "aiming" and "trying," and start trusting your new skill with the Magic Triangle.

ON THE PUTTING GREEN

HERE'S WHERE so many hopes die when they could be happily fulfilled. The old mechanical method breaks down under pressure, but the intuitive triangle we've been talking about just gets better.

How many times have you seen players drop several balls on

the practice green and hit the same putt over and over? Getting the groove, right? Also getting rigor mortis and further dampening their ability to respond to changing situations and create the unique shot needed out on the course.

On the putting green you have a limited number of targets, but by constantly moving the ball around, each cup becomes a different target so to speak. So . . . first warm up your stroke and get the feel of the green for a few minutes.

Then start your real practicing by hitting totally different putts every time. First, a ten-footer, for example. Then a left-breaking twenty-five-footer, then a downhill breaking four-footer, than an uphill straight-in fourteen-footer . . . you get the idea.

Varying the distances and types of putts keeps you out of conditioned ruts. It also keeps your Magic Triangle resource freshly tuned, flexible and increasingly effective as it learns to respond instantly to new requirements.

We're developing spontaneous intuitive precision here, not automated conditioned reflexes.

Play around with this exercise on the putting green and follow the Magic Triangle rules to a tee. Be willing to goof up a bit, as one does when learning anything new. You won't be goofing for long, I assure you. (For the *coup de grâce* of putting, see the next exercise, *The Target Is Locked!*)

ON THE GOLF COURSE

HERE'S WHERE it all pays off. On the course, every shot is new, every target different. See why we've been practicing always with a different target?

From tee to green, you should now be used to having only one shot at one target. Thus, the tension that usually builds up when we try to remember everything we did to get that perfect shot after hitting twenty-seven range balls at the same target . . . you notice it's hardly there anymore. We're used to being in new territory every time—*creating*, rather than reacting—just like we were in practice.

Remember: Don't try. Just do.
- Clearly identify your target.
- Quickly, thoroughly visualize your shot happening.
- *Know* your Magic Triangle has you perfectly programmed to connect with your target.
- Don't aim *at* target. Connect *with* it.
- Relax and swing away.

For the time and attention you invest, the Magic Triangle will return some magic golf for as long as you swing with it.

A NOTE ON THE DRIVER & FAIRWAY WOODS: Ever wondered why the driver is, with rare exception, the most wayward, inconsistent club in your bag? Of course, it's because we're hot-blooded macho types and we want to whale away and hit it 300 yards. Swing real hard just in case you hit it.

Those slices, pulls, snap hooks and worm-killing scudders are all the proof you need that we should start treating the woods (metals) like any other club: give it a specific target to

An old carpenter once taught me the secret of driving nails (and saving my thumb): "Watch the hole it's making, not the head of the nail. You'll never miss."

Thousands of nails later and still counting, I can confirm he was absolutely right.

shoot at. That target should be a good twenty-five yards shorter than you think you can easily hit it.

Do it, and your drives will be going consistently straighter and—don't be too surprised—much longer.

When the chief of the archery contest

asked Arjuna what he saw before him,

Arjuna replied,

"I see the eye of the fish."

The Target Is Locked!

AT ANY GIVEN MOMENT, ALL THE FORCES OF NATURE SWEEP
IN TO PLAY AT THE POINT OF OUR UNDIVIDED ATTENTION.

ABOUT THIS EXERCISE

HERE WE ARE in the cockpit with Clint Eastwood as he
streaks away from a secret Siberian air base in the super-high-
tech jet fighter he's just stolen from the Soviets. But their top
pilot soon scrambles an identical fighter and is hot on Clint's
vapor trail. He finally catches up and struggles desperately to
lock in on Clint with his radar target-detection system and nail
him with an air-to-air missile strike.

But Clint is the wily veteran and, of course, much smarter than
his younger hormone-riddled adversary. Clint dives, turns and

pulls out every trick he knows until finally he wearies of toying with this nuisance on his tail. Clint squints and his eyes turn to icy blue steel as he commands the sophisticated voice-activated target-locking system to identify and fire at his pesky pursuer.

Suddenly, the target is locked! Clint's backside missile now streaks into the intake port of the Soviet ace's fighter. Varoom! A fiery explosion fills the air as the enemy plane disintegrates and falls away in a million fragments of flaming steel and flesh.

His day made, Clint banks hard away from the rapidly sinking wreckage, a rueful grin on his weathered face as he checks yet another threat to the free world off his long list.

I always wanted to thank Clint for all the times he's saved America and made our city streets safe.

But what I really want to tell him is how much I appreciate the profound putting lesson he gave me in that climactic closing scene of *Firefox*. I'll send him a complimentary copy of this book as a totally inadequate but very sincere token of my gratitude.

> A single cell in the human body is doing about six trillion things per second. (The body) can play music, kill germs, make a baby, recite poetry, and monitor the movement of stars all at the same time. . . .
>
> —DEEPAK CHOPRA

That's right . . . putting lesson. Lock the target and fire.

Clint's movie jet, and all the real fighter planes in the world, represent billions of dollars and research into precision electronic target-tracking systems. But each of us owns an infinitely better system. Right here between our shoulder blades.

By far, the most sophisticated and untapped technology on this planet is the human spirit-electromagnetic-bio-system organic unit. Its power source is the heart and its computer data processing center is the brain.

The human heart and brain have been languishing in near dormancy for æons, longing to be used in some exciting, creative ways. Something a bit more challenging than making to-do lists, fretting about the future, and channel scanning. Booooring! Well, why not get them to do something really important, like sink a few putts, just for starters?

The time is now. We're on the verge of an awesome new dimension in putting, golf in general, and anywhere else you want to apply this amazing exercise.

You Are the System

PURPOSE: To develop and use your own precise target lock-and-fire system.

MATERIALS: Putter and balls at first. Other clubs soon after.

DURATION: Three times (or more) a week for six weeks minimum.

SETTING: Carpet at home or office, putting green.

THIS IS NOT a quick-fix gimmick, but rather a sustained training exercise to bring you long-term results. It may seem like a lot of steps now, and in the early stages each one should be taken carefully. But soon each step will occur almost automatically, and *the whole process shouldn't take more than a few seconds.*

If it takes any longer, you're thinking too much and your effectiveness will decrease markedly while your golfing buddies yawn impatiently.

BASIC RULES OF THIS EXERCISE:

* Understand that you are—and may use anytime you like—the most advanced computing system on this planet.

- As you survey each shot, see yourself as feeding all relevant data into your computer, into the highly sophisticated target detection and locking system at your disposal.
- Tell yourself that you are perfectly computing all necessary data that will send precise instructions to your body to create the perfect shot. You don't need to think about anything beyond that.

Here's the procedure. Adapt it to suit your preferences, but stay within the basic rules:

1) Just before you address the ball, pulse a radar beam from your eye going out to identify the target: anything in the room or any cup on the putting green. See it hit the target with a bright white flash about the size of a golf ball and say to yourself: "The target is identified."

2) Now set up to your ball: hands soft, arms firm but limber, comfortably balanced, relaxed, set. Take a practice stroke or two for feel and distance. Then set the putter head on line with the target as you normally would.

3) As you set up to the ball, picture the Magic Triangle connecting the eyes, ball, and target. Don't stand there and try to draw the triangle—*it's already present, so just recognize it.* See it appear instantly without trying.

    I visualize the triangle as intense purple laser beams converging at its three points: eye, ball, target. The laser beams are feeding my computer all the necessary data to do the job.

4) Now, as you're visualizing the triangle, pulse a high-intensity light strobe directly down the laser beam that connects your eye to the target. See this pulse as a white-light blast, the size of a golf ball, that hits the target center and instantly bounces back to your eye.

Make it like the piercing strobe lights on a highway patrol car that just pulled over a vanload of teenagers. However you do it, just quickly strobe the target and see it light up.

5) When the target is "lit"—which should

It became way easier to chop wood for my stove when I focused on where my axe blade would *finish*, rather than where it would enter the wood.

Martial arts master Bruce Lee always focused on where his punch would finish. In golf, use this principle by focusing primarily on the target, not the striking of the ball.

take just a second or two at most—know that the returning light strobe is feeding your computer the precise information it needs to give you a perfect shot. Say firmly to yourself, "The target is locked!"

6) With only the image of the lit target in your mind, look down at the ball and smoothly stroke it. Don't aim! Don't think! Just stroke smoothly and let the putter head follow through toward the target. Your head must remain absolutely still during the stroke.

You may notice how your hands *automatically* begin to set the clubface to the exact angle required *without any conscious effort on your part*. Let the hands remain soft and free to respond to your system's slightest impulses. Any "thinking" at all will tighten your hands, pull them out of their perfect alignment and fudge the shot.

After you practice this exercise for a week or so, the whole process should take no more than five to six seconds. *The longer you take, the more likely you are to mess up the shot.* Don't hurry, but don't go into brain lock either.

When Clint activated his firing mechanism, he didn't need to talk the missile to the target. Once it was locked on, the system knew how to do its job quite well, thank you. Let *your* system go on autopilot and take it home from there.

Trust is the key idea here. Like faith, trust only works if you go all the way, one hundred percent with it. Anything less gives you a mixed-up mind and mixed results.

This is a seemingly "aimless" but incredibly precise method that, when you develop and trust it sufficiently, will reveal the perfect system you've always had waiting within yourself.

What's to prevent it from being so? Only your meddling thoughts that say it can't—nothing else! Isn't that awesome to know?

PRECISE TARGET ALIGNMENT

USE A variation of this method for precise target alignment, especially out on the course where you can't lay clubs down in front of you as directional guides. This can work for every shot, tee to green. Here's how:

- Pick an exact target for *every* shot. Set up to the ball and align yourself in the general direction of the target.
- As in the putting exercise, strobe your target and *hold your focus there*—keep the target "lit."
- As you focus intently on your "lit" target, adjust your position until you *feel* lined up and comfortable. Then look down on your golf ball and swing away.

You're going to be amazed.

EVEN IF OUR EFFORTS OF ATTENTION SEEM FOR YEARS

TO BE PRODUCING NO RESULT,

ONE DAY A LIGHT IN EXACT PROPORTION TO THEM

WILL FLOOD THE SOUL.

—Simone Weil

Holes in Your Head

DREAMS ARE PLACES WE GO, FREE OF THE BODY'S RESTRAINTS,
TO PLAY WITH THE REST OF OURSELVES.

ABOUT THIS EXERCISE

EVERY DAY, AFTER morning roll call and the usual breakfast of watery rice gruel, he worked his way back to his personal space in the straw hut. He anticipated this time with great relish, when he could withdraw into his thoughts and leave behind, for a time, the awful truth that he was a captive, now going on two years, in a North Vietnamese prison camp.

He'd since gotten over the initial shock of being captured after ejecting from his crippled aircraft and parachuting into the jungles of the Demilitarized Zone near the border between North and South Vietnam.

He had slowly grown numb after weeks of heart-wrenching despair and disbelief that he was actually trapped in the squalor of this prison camp hellhole. It seemed like a lifetime since he'd known the exhilarating freedom as an air force pilot jetting high above the dotted landscape below. Unknowingly, he'd overflown dozens of these prison camps with only a distant idea of the misery and pain languishing in them. They had all looked like tiny ants far away down there . . . and now he was one of the ants.

After an aimless "exercise" stroll around the small compound and some routine chitchat with fellow prisoners, he now sat cross-legged on the floor of his hut, his back resting against the bamboo wall support. He knew he wouldn't be bothered here. The camp guards wanted nothing but his silence and docility, which he had learned to give them after those first few weeks of being tormented and roughed around, after his fruitless pleading for better food, cleaner water, medicine, tools, books, sanitary living conditions.

Everything had soon settled into a dull, deadening routine of nowhere to go, nothing to do, and only a dying ember of hope that someday, somehow they could all go home. What to do when there is nothing to do?

He sat and began breathing evenly and deeply. His mind became still in the steady rhythm of air flowing in and out of him. He gradually had trained his mind, once a turmoil of pesky and unruly thoughts, to instantly obey his slightest wish. He could imagine whatever he wanted to appear on the screen of his mind more quickly than one could change channels on a television set.

He had developed an ability to create any new program he

wanted to watch—or participate in—in precise detail. He became the producer, the script, the scenes, the actor and audience of any show he chose to imagine. He thus developed a tremendous inner power in an outwardly powerless place.

By the time he'd entered active duty, he was a low-handicapper. His travels with the air force allowed him to play a wide range of interesting and exotic golf courses around the world. He remembered many of them, and now, with all this time and nowhere to go, he started reflecting on some of his favorite rounds and favorite courses.

With nothing more pressing on his schedule, he'd begun to create another world for himself in the fertile seeding ground of his imagination, where he was absolutely free to do whatever he pleased. With his increasingly refined imagining abilities and mental control, he began to play an "inner" round of golf every day at the course of his choice.

Not just swinging a few shots on some vaguely remembered holes, these became total, complete rounds of golf. Undisturbed in the quietude of his hut, he clearly pictured himself in every detail: calling up for a tee time, driving to the course, getting the clubs out of the car, lacing up his golf shoes, checking in at the pro shop, hitting balls on the range, strolling over to the first tee, looking over the scorecard and noting the shape and yardage of the first hole, pulling the driver out of the bag, pulling its club cover off, reaching into his pocket for a tee, tossing up a few blades of grass to test the breeze, taking a couple of practice swings, imagining the shot.

Now get set, a couple of waggles, swing back and then through, feel and hear the click of that ball springing off the sweet spot, watch it split the fairway and come to rest about

265 yards out there. Now that felt good! The next shot was equally satisfying, and so was the next one. . . .

Unbeknownst to his captors, some great rounds of golf were being played all over the world from there inside that grungy hut in the prison camp. Day in and day out, golf course to golf course, never shooting over his handicap and often shooting under it, he played and played. He was quoted later as saying that his daily rounds of golf were all that kept him from going insane. (Sorta works that way out here, too.) His swing was smooth and strong. His short game was better than ever. He rarely missed anything under ten feet on the greens.

> Keep your hands open, and
>
> all the sands of the desert
>
> can pass through them.
>
> Close them, and all you
>
> can feel is a bit of grit.
>
> —TAISEN DESHIMARU

Then one day, after more than five years in captivity, they opened the gates and set him free. He was taken to a special re-orientation center for debriefing and counseling as he began the process of returning to normal life. Then an air force transport flew him home to the United States, where, with his family and friends, he would hope to pick up where he left off years earlier.

He faced a long road to recovery from malnutrition, disease, and the mental and emotional trauma of captivity. He was physically emaciated and thirty pounds underweight.

Yet within a few weeks after he touched down on American soil—without having picked up a golf club for several years— he played a "real" round of golf on one of those courses he had imagined so often in his little prison hut. Incredibly, he shot a 76.

"ALL YOUR 'SELVES' ARE EXHAUSTED AND GONE.

NOW: HIT THE BALL WITH WHAT IS LEFT."

JUNAH'S GLANCE WAS DESPERATE.

"BUT THERE'S *NOTHING* LEFT."

VANCE NODDED. "EXACTLY."

The Perfect Round of Golf

PURPOSE: To train the mind/body to act out the best golf game imaginable.

MATERIALS: A willing heart and a keen desire to re-discover your power.

DURATION: Two-week sessions. Then as much as you like.

WHERE: At home or wherever you won't be disturbed for a while.

WELL, WHO'S GOT time to sit around everyday and imagine playing a whole round of golf? Hey, I hardly even get time to play once a week. Sometimes it seems like we're in jail, but this is a hyper-busy one with little or no time for lounging about and playing dream games.

So how to make use of this incredible power of imagination when we're jamming on the All-American diet of hurry up and get somewhere so we can hurry up and get somewhere else?

Not to worry. Let's take the big movie and divide it into little frames that anyone can do anytime. Even in a ten-minute exercise, we can plant the seeds that will blossom into big results and so much lunch money they could name a table after you at the club.

Let's start with just one club and take a trip to the Dreamland Driving Range. It's an ideal place . . . the balls are free, it's not crowded, the sun's shining on your back as a barely perceptible breeze keeps your skin temperature just right. Imagine a few decorative clouds if you like—cumulus, cirrus, mackerel scales, take your pick. Nobody here to bother you with a boring shot-by-shot replay of their last two rounds.

Go ahead, imagine this driving range just the way you like it. After all, this is your private place in your private world, and you can do absolutely any blessed thing you want here! Where else can you have it this good?

Okay, let's get to work, if you want to call this work. Give the following some focus every day for a couple of weeks and see what happens:

1) Pick a time and place where you're not likely to be disturbed. This takes a little concentration so, unless you're a meditation guru, the fewer distractions the better. Ten minutes before bed is the optimum time because your fresh imaginings follow you to dreamland. There, undisturbed in the stillness of a night's sleep, they'll permeate your energy patterns more thoroughly.

2) Breathe slowly, deeply, and clear your screen. Now imagine our perfect Dreamland Driving Range in just enough detail to be standing here next to your bag of clubs. Just picture yourself here and keep it simple for now. More detail as you get better at this.

3) Now pick a club out of the bag. How about a pitching wedge? We all need to get it closer to the pin so we can have something besides long chips or thirty-five-foot birdie putts.

Look at your wedge a moment—the grip, the shaft,

the head, the grooves. Heft it and feel its weight and balance. How many grooves are carved into the club face? Count them now as best you can.

4) Swing it a few times, taking a nice, strong, easy, flowing swing. No hurry, you're on dream time here. *Don't think technique.* Think only flow of movement and perfect results.

Your obedient subconscious energy field will take care of all the details. Just think how you want this to feel . . . and *feel* it.

5) Pick some random targets—always different ones——and take some shots at them. Imagine your strong, flowing swing meeting the ball perfectly. Feel that compression right on the sweet spot, the sound we all want to hear coming off the clubface. Now watch the ball loft out there and finish *exactly* on your target. Great shot! Work through a dozen or so balls this way.

Be alert for thoughts that would disrupt your satisfying shotmaking—*don't give them even a second of energy.* If they persist, load those suckers in the Black Ball and tap 'em into the blue-fire cup as in *Who's Calling Your Shots?* Get your attention right back to making perfect shots, and keep it here!

6) Close your practice session by putting the club back in the bag. You should be feeling pretty good about your swing and the way the ball behaved just as you wanted it to.

These sessions can be with one or more clubs on the range. Or play a hole or two . . . or a whole round if you really get into it. Visualize as much detail as you like—the more you refine these imaginary actions, the deeper they'll work into your subconscious and thus into your real game.

In some ways, practice in your imagination can be as good or better at developing a great golf game than the real thing. You can make yourself, your club, your golf ball do whatever you want during these sessions.

Imagination programs our subconscious mind, where images of everything we've experienced—in thought, feeling, visualizing—are stored and *are constantly acting through us.*

Our subconscious mind-field doesn't care what we feed it. It is totally impartial and unconcerned whether we quadruple bogey or eagle. Its job simply is to act out the beliefs and images we've allowed to abide in our awareness—which it has been doing, incidentally, since time began.

How we play magical golf in the physical world depends on the focus we apply to playing these magical holes in our head—along with the images we hold of who we are and what we believe is possible.

IMPORTANT: What we do at the Dreamland Driving Range becomes an active, living part of us—so don't get sloppy. Imagine only what you really want and be meticulous about it, because whatever you picture starts growing in you. Wow!

Postscript

IF YOU'VE MADE it straight through to here, I can just
imagine what you're thinking: Okay, now what do I do with all
this wacky stuff? Since this book started filtering through me
more than five years ago, I've been asking myself that same
question. And I keep getting the same answer, in a variety of
ways: Stay awake and pay attention, PB! You've been creating
your life since the day you were born. Now start doing it *consciously* instead of unconsciously.

As many of us know, "staying awake" is one of life's great
challenges. Every day the world offers up hundreds of excuses
and ways for me to close down and go heart-dead on my feet,
to duck out on personal responsibility for how I see and relate
to everything in my life. But that's its job, to show us that our
perceived problems and solutions are within, not to be found
anywhere out here in the nuthouse of human activity. The
world we see is the *result*, not the cause of our condition.

My old pals, the cosmic laws, also have taught me that life
boils down to two fundamental activities: Create or react. When
we're awake we create. When we're asleep we react (replaying the
past instead of moving on with our lives). When I stay awake,

especially during the last split second when clubhead meets the ball, my odds of a good shot increase immensely. When I cave in to the almost overwhelming tendency to blank out at the moment of impact, it seems like the accumulated disasters of the world rush into this void and try to take over my shot. When you get close to the moment of truth (I keep telling myself), stay awake and look it in the eye! You'll meet another part of yourself that's trying to reconnect with you—like the sweet spot on your clubface, and all the other faces you encounter.

But maybe the most powerful lesson I'm learning from this book—which I also credit for shaving six strokes off my handicap so far—is: I am a product of my own self-image, my gut feelings about who I am and what I'm doing here. Self-image is the primary heart/mind filter that processes all information entering my awareness, and all expressions coming out of it. From deep within, these soul-driven beliefs run the show from start to finish. It's taken a while to understand that I'm the one who created all my filters—and I'm always free to make any kind I want. The implications here are scary yet very liberating!

Wouldn't you know, my own book is a huge homework assignment that may take the rest of my life and then some. I hope it's offered up one or two nutritious ideas for your soul palate. It's all about the thrills and spills of staying awake. Falling down. Getting back up. Enjoying the endless opportunities life offers us on our magnificent adventure of self-creation. I feel reassured knowing we're all working on this together, in our own ways. Thanks, and bless our birdies and bogies alike. They both have a lot to teach us.

To contact the author, write to:
Printer Bowler, PO Box 9292, Missoula, MT 59807